I0470347

Stormy Fortune

Cover painting by Andrew Goldfarb [xx]
Written by Shawn Michael Sullivan

Neon Burrito Publishing 🔥 13

Copyright 2017

BISAC: Art / Individual Artists / Essays
ISBN: 9780998520537

Also by Shawn Michael Sullivan
Available from Neon Burrito

Novella

Larry Angeles

Novelette

My Autobiography Is My Manifesto: Volume One [8.5x11"]
^ *automanifest* [5x8"]

A novelette plus two fragments and a bonus adult-kids book

Oscar Wilde's The Picture of Dorian Gray

Short stories w/Morgan Drolet

Cosmic Robotics

Poetry w/Alessandra and Florianne Rizzotti

Everything Within

Poetry w/Morgan Drolet

Frank Zappa & Barry Manilow 2014
the name of this book is untitled but that's a bit of a lie 2015
Eudaimonia 2016
Baker's Dozen 2017
Basic Mutant Psychosis 2014-2016 Collection

CONTENTS

Can something that everyone must undergo be a cause of misery to one?

Cicero, *On Living and Dying Well*

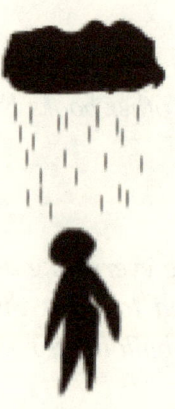

How absurd—and a complete stranger to the world—is the man surprised at any aspect of his experience in life!

Marcus Aurelius, *Meditations*

Chapter One

A perspective on the history and future of humans, zooming into contemporary Los Angeles existence.

Back before everything established these days, including the concept of days, back before science, back before poetry, no poetry, goddamn... here you are before language, when ineffability was everything, you are here. Imagine. Your higher consciousness is new to this old planet. You know not a name for your hands but your hands are yours you know, and you cannot explain your head or your heart but you can see an animal which is now extinct. *Pretty cool.* And what you do is what humans do: live by day and dream by night.

For humans only: creating models of the universe within one's mind; conceiving of reality from an objective perspective; conceptualizing one's interior; implementing reason and sometimes guessing while feeling emotional. The universe had/has/always will have life's ingredients, but only humans write its recipes.

Today's humans possess an elevated concept of cosmic awareness—and yet still they don't know where they're headed toward or coming from. Fact: contemporary humans who act as if they live in the future and know everything are hilarious because every day is ephemeral within eternity, and we do not know nearly everything. What's tragic is we know our Sun one day will die. And Earth, our first love, all we have known so far, it may die before the Sun. This will be a tremendous life obstacle, but it is surmountable, based on evidence from human history, science, and the abstract concept of belief. Forever: strange land becomes new land we live upon. Fingers crossed that a cataclysm doesn't destroy human civilization.

From a perspective of humans living forever, some day one day this day will have taken place upon a dead planet in the far-flung past. So how does today matter, among that many days? Like this: yesterday happened for today; today happened for tomorrow.

In terms of what's known of the history of existence, it's known that it's rather mind boggling really. No one can make contact with the last universal common ancestor. Narrowing down to humans: still mind boggling. Neither the Mitochondrial Eve nor the Y-chromosomal Adam have been discovered. A gorgeous phylogenetic tree indicates abundant human migration spanning time, but the human path to the Americas is an enormous scientific mystery, with archeological records of initial sites submerged beneath the rising waters of an unstable Pacific coastline, creating uncertainties related to potential human migration over the Beringian land bridge and/or coastal migration across the Pacific Ocean.

But this world is as it is, and the mental task which requires thoughts of another world is this: imagine if the Americas were never once discovered by anybody, nobody ever stepped foot on the Americas, throughout the entire past and future of humans on Earth. If that were reality, then, there being less known of the exterior world, would humans know less of themselves—and the real question is: are we always the same as we are, unrelated to what we do or do not know of our world?

In reality, one-third the total population of Native Americans lived in the land that became California. The highest population density of its time: hunter-gatherers; practitioners of religion; practitioners of hallucinogenics; developers of unique cultures, such as the La Jolla Complex and the Pauma Complex; explorers of possibilities within human existence; explorers of personal meaning within a sense of being.

The name of California first appeared in a romantic novel written by Garci Rodríguez de Montalvo, read by Spanish conquistadors, and included within Don Quixote's library, *Las sergas de Esplandián* (*The Exploits of Esplandián*):

> Know that on the right hand from the Indies exists an
> island called California very close to a side of the
> Earthly Paradise; and it was populated by black
> women, without any man existing there, because they
> lived in the way of the Amazons.

The mutineer Fortún Ximénez first landed a ship upon the land believed to be ruled by Queen Calafia. At first on maps the Baja California Peninsula was *the island of California.*

In a later reality a northern portion of this land became Alta California, the Tongva people became Gabrieleños and Fernandeños, living among the Diegueños, Luiseños, Juaneños —and people of Spanish ancestry migrated here as pobladores, becoming Californios who lived, for example, in El Pueblo de

Nuestra Señora la Reina de los Ángeles (The Town of Our Lady the Queen of the Angels). In this context ranchos flourished in Los Angeles to such an extent that, after Mexico won against Spain their War of Independence, then amid manifest destiny, after the Siege of Los Angeles, after the United States captured California, later during the Gold Rush, this pueblo became known as Queen of the Cow Counties.

A Mexican land grant, Rancho La Brea, transformed into new names upon American real estate maps, in this city where land was gold. The name for Hollywood was said to have first appeared in the honeymoon minds of Mr. and Mrs. Whitley. But the Mother of Hollywood was Daeida Wilcox Beveridge, born in Hicksville, Ohio. She and her husband placed Hollywood on a map. She named Sunset Boulevard. She installed Hollywood's first sidewalk in front of her home on Prospect Avenue, which became Hollywood Boulevard after the city of Hollywood merged with Los Angeles (for its aqueducts).

It was plain well-known that early moviemakers adored the paradisiacal weather of Hollywood. The first movie shot in Hollywood was a Latino melodrama, *In Old California*, a period piece set in days when Mexico owned California. Its director D.W. Griffith returned to New York City with news of this wondrous land; quite similar to the information of Queen

Calafia's land being discovered by Fortún Ximénez, in terms of cultural imagination having a direct impact upon emerging landscapes. Movies were a science, an industry, an art. Movies were portholes into possibilities and people across the globe peered inside. Hollywood became a Dream Factory within a country made by and for dreams. Hollywood reestablished The American Dream, for when reality would kill dreams, as reality often would, movies would grant them life again.

Back in the past and today in the present, south of Hollywood are the La Brea Tar Pits. These days there is Park La Brea, the largest housing development in the U.S. west of the Mississippi River. This is Wilshire District, which is called Mid-City West. Here there is Miracle Mile, with its Museum Row. Here there is Carthay Circle: true. And here there is what became, after WWII, the center for Jewish settlement within Los Angeles: Fairfax District. The past, present, and future of Los Angeles stretch back and reach forward in ways dependent upon the distinct reality of each citizen, in whose chest and head the raw materials of dreams are stored, so in Fairfax District is The Raoul Wallenberg Square, which is named for a provider of protective passports to Jewish Hungarian citizens during the Holocaust; always: the best thing is for reality to come from hope. A hope is a dream. Movies and dreams are equal since movies are dreams. All movies and dreams are lighter than reality. Always we hope. This is the philosophy of Los Angeles which assists the everyday.

Fairfax District is south of West Hollywood, which is its own glorious microcosm, wherein Sunset Strip grew, this city-in-a-city that was initially named Sherman, by its founder Moses Sherman, but a realty business inspired its change. This book was written in an apartment on the second floor of a Spanish Revival home, one street back and one street over from The Raoul Wallenberg Square, therefore outside the limits of Fairfax District, and south of West Hollywood, within Beverly Grove.

The name Beverly Grove is a realty concoction which references two neighborhood malls: Beverly Center and The Grove. This is next to Beverly Hills, below which is Beverlywood. Beverly Grove has not yet established its own distinct cultural identity. It has Cedars-Sinai Medical Center, with its holy name. During the time this book is being written, in relation to diverse ethnic potentials within the city of Los Angeles, Beverly Grove is not especially diverse. Though its percentages of never-married men and women are among the county's highest. This is a neighborhood creating its own identity within the shadows of history. This is a neighborhood building its own character, and it can do it if it does it, by pulling itself by its bootstraps, which is the way one does it.

Here are ecstatic essays written from Beverly Grove, since humans write what history becomes, as the beginning of this chapter mentioned in another way. And all this is possible because life squeezes inside of words the same as life squeezes inside a city, plus this city and these words were co-written by dreams, so with those two factors combined, that's how all this is possible.

Chapter Two

My early life history, emphasis on beginning to daydream in Ohio; sentimental.

Toward the end of the twentieth century, when I was born, everything was embarrassing (it still is). Everybody wanted to know of tomorrow (they still do). Everybody was figuring out how to be anybody (they still are). Anything seemed possible and people who were messes were only human (things were different back then).

I wasn't born research, I was born normal-style, as a fucking human. I was born and bred not oceanic but continental: a Midwestern American. In my youth I learned that people are the earth and the earth is good, and this place and these people were all I first knew and loved. My belief in people and dreams comes from The Heart of It All, Ohio. This chapter is dedicated to my mother and sister. Both my sister and I had fathers named Michael. I was Shawn Michael Sullivan and she was Melinda MacDonald, eleven years between us, our mother was Donna Hinders.

Donna met my father while he was a truck driver and she was a grocery store manager. They never married nor lived together. They never loved each other. My mother raised me with her maternal instincts. I would see my father about once a month on a weekend. He became a used car salesman while I was young, when everyone made jokes about used car salesmen being terrible people who lied to make their lives better. Then my father told me he sold all the cars in the lot, and he became a public bus driver in downtown Dayton. He was a bus driver until he retired. Then for some time after he retired he did very little. But the weight of being alone and doing very little pushed down on his psychological state of being. So some time after he retired as a bus driver he found other low-paying jobs, such as at Wal-Mart, but he did not stay there, even after he had been employee of the month in his department, for he didn't keep one same job for too long after he retired as a bus driver and continued searching for himself within The Blue Collar Dream.

My family was a mixed breed of European nations, but our family tree disappeared inside the Appalachian Mountains. I knew that my last name sounded Irish. My father once bought me a sweatshirt with a family crest, which my mother explained was bullshit from the mall. My mother's father had been a milk man. My mother's mother was a beautician who became a restaurant owner; I called her my grandmother. My mother was one of six children, along with Sherry, Cathy, Cindy, Mike, and Julie. I had thirteen cousins. Donna's was a baby boomer family, her father had served in WWII, as had my grandmother's second husband (whom I called my grandfather). My grandfather was a security guard who twice won five-digit lottery tickets. He and my grandmother lived and worked in downtown Dayton. When I was a child, while my single mother worked, I spent nights sleeping at my grandparents' house. Like this—

I'm on a brass-framed guest room bed. The room is decorated with nostalgic trinkets of an emotionally delectable variety. Moonlight shines through the windows. Here I lie, put to bed by my grandmother, with no particular thought in my mind, except *Nice*. What from the world can hurt me I don't wonder,

I don't worry since I am young and the world hasn't shown me pain. Night I do not fear for it is a quieter version of the same world I know by day. In fact, the quietness of nighttime is my favorite. Based on me not really listening to sounds during the day. Days are too loud, too bright, too everything. *Forget about it*! All I need is what's in the night: barely anything and only my favorites. All I need from the light of the sun is its reflection off the moon. *Thank you*. And none of that is what I'm thinking tucked inside the brass-framed bed. Now I'm asleep. But then I'm shortly awakened by a hallway light shining behind my grandfather. He takes off his uniform. He comes and lies beside me. We fall asleep together now.

It was my understanding that being at my grandparent's house was the best place to be. Their home was a chamber of life possibility, I was sure. Such texture, I felt. I was often there or at my grandmother's restaurant, Mom's Here Food Service. Mom's Here Food Service was decorated by an immense accumulation of tokens accrued from my grandparents' long lives, and I was a child with the world opening in front of me. It was there amid so many possible feelings where for my first time I experienced a sourceless feeling. One time what happened was I walked through Mom's Here Food Service and my thoughts held a mild sensation without a cause which I could determine—a feeling in my thoughts perhaps not from some actual moment of my life. I couldn't reach the root of a certain flower inside my mind and I wondered if an emotional seed had ricocheted off a wall, ricocheted off a Norman Rockwell painting into my garden of thoughts some days ago and grown there as if I had planted it. This inextricable and curious sensation I would encounter again and again through life: not of deja vu, but its sticky residue. That was unusual and most times what happened was I would sit on a wooden table in my grandmother's restaurant and she would bring me a plate of her family-famous BEPCs. Bacon, eggs, potato, cheese. And I remember walking the kitchen while my grandmother cooked an order, walking outside onto the back patio, past my grandfather smoking a cigar, to the edge of their lot where I pondered. I gazed down the sidewalk and across the street and considered all the things I knew and all the things I didn't know. I would see a person on the sidewalk, and I had never seen that before person. All the people I knew and all the people I didn't know. I wanted to know more of life, more of what I knew and what I didn't know. My grandparents familiarized me with life's intricate complexities. For example, my grandmother told me that smoking cigars was leading my grandfather toward blindness, according to a doctor. This she told me one early evening across a dinner table as my grandfather smoked a cigar before leaving for work. This was me learning about what life can do and does, about good and bad choices. My grandfather would soon go blind, but he didn't quit smoking cigars. And I didn't begin to think that smoking cigars made him blind, but my grandmother taught me how to make a dramatic point, which was one of my family's strongest and most endearing qualities, in our opinion.

And my grandparents taught me how to watch television at night, treating television as distance and perspective from life's harsh realities. My grandparents taught me a tender chorus of grace which goes, *Feeling light, dreaming // Know why I should // Don't know why I shouldn't,* which is from the song of pop culture.

Dayton was the birthplace of aviation, and it was almost my birthplace. I was born in its most populated suburb, Kettering, which was named after an inventor of the electrical starting motor and some various other things which were tremendous, lasting ideas. I first lived in an apartment. I had a bedroom but I often slept with my mother, since that was much better than sleeping alone, I felt. Donna dreamed of other things besides being a grocery store manager. She wanted to explore other parts of herself and the world. She became employed at Matchmaker International, and from there she selected who became my stepfather. At Matchmaker what happened was a person paid to be interviewed by a Matchmaker employee (like my mother), the employee would fill out a card about the person, and dates would be arranged between people whose cards suggested favorable results. My stepfather had expressed to Matchmaker that he didn't want to date someone with children. That box was checked on his card. But when they met he came to love my mother as she guessed he would. *Nailed it!* Two weeks after they met he proposed. We moved from our Kettering apartment to his Beavercreek house. Melinda and I were accessories to their marriage, and what would become of us we didn't know, since we were young. But I didn't feel afraid. I had my own room in this house with its two stories and a chill basement, staircases and hallways and everything here a family thing. I lived an imitation of The Family Dream. My stepfather didn't speak to me often, and when he did he used a soft voice. He was not mean. He only once ever spanked me, and it was embarrassing for us both, I felt even back then. What had I done? Something naughty no doubt. My sister was in high school at the time of the marriage. I was entering kindergarten. As a family we ran forward with our hands raised in the wind, smiles on our faces.

Following marriage, running forward in her life, my mother opened a Matchmaker International franchise in Lexington, Kentucky. She would bring me with her now and then. Reality there felt separate from reality in Beavercreek. Mostly the same, but small differences which meant a great deal. Alone by myself outside Matchmaker International at night in Lexington, I learned to wonder-walk alone but unafraid, which would become my lifestyle. My stream of wonder was a result of both my consciousness and this world being so enormous, seriously. There it was: Lexington, Kentucky. There I was. At night out alone I absorbed the humongous feeling of being alive in Lexington and that was a treat for me and my emotions back then plus always, because that's who I was, receptive to places strange to me and familiar to others. There was a diner in Lexington which was the first diner I treasured, a '50s themed diner with a purple neon sign that said *Since 1992.*

Matchmaker became a financial success the year my mother's father died. She thanked him. Our family moved into a home we built in Bellbrook. This new house would be on country roads outside the 'burbs, away from the masses, where we could mind our own business and live our own lives on our own land. The Country Dream. A Darling Dream. Another subsection of The American Dream. Our neighborhood's name was a realty invention: River Ridge. Mostly River Ridge was populated by young money. Most lawns were sodded grass with a few random trees, although one retired couple lived with an immaculately constructed lawn that was far different from the yards around them, theirs being this crafty dish with these neat touches which they designed for the enjoyment of their final days in their country home. Their gardens had style, the only gardens with style in the whole damn place. But most of the neighborhood population forged fresh dreams, their lawns were yards and portions of their dreams only in terms of how large and country they were. Many houses were owned by doctors. My stepfather worked for the United States Air Force and took a long commute to Wright Patterson in Beavercreek. I became friends with nearby River Ridge children, mostly boys. Through my entire time there, as new people moved in and as I aged, there were eleven neighborhood children with whom I became friends, and eight of them were boys. Half of them lived in a house across the street from mine. The father of those four boys was an anesthesiologist. He worked at the Seventh-day Adventist Kettering Hospital (where I was born). His wife would convince my mother to send me to the Seventh-day Adventist private school Spring Valley Academy, which I would attend from sixth grade until high school graduation, experiencing just three days of Bellbrook public high school my junior year. In the bubble of an Ohio country youth I dreamed of the big wide world and my future self I would become, believing that the world was big and wide and I could become somebody. That just made sense to me. That was what Ohio believed: anybody could become somebody. I couldn't think of why that wouldn't be true. Not back then. Our house was atop a hill. I would gaze across the hill at the Community Center next to the Little Miami River. Life was all around me, it was immense and I was within it.

Too, I knew of the world's immensity through fond visits to the local bookstore, Books & Co. Being ready for anything was first taught to me by R.L. Stein. Later but still young, Stephen King and Michael Crichton would expand this idea. I was raised in part by books and movies and music, the glow of television, long and lonely nights on Midwestern country roads. Before I became an adult who took long walks across sidewalks as a means of traveling within my thoughts, as a developing teenager I played videogames and listened to music. Though my reality never appeared similar to anything in popular entertainment. In general there wasn't often harmony between my thoughts and the world. But in my youth I speculated that life would be chiller if it were more like *Super Mario 64*.

One snowy day when I was a freshman in high school I was ready to be baptized as a Seventh-day Adventist. This religion practiced late baptism. But heavy snow canceled my first baptism plan. My Kentucky cousin Paul had visited for my baptism, but also because we were cousins who were friends, so after that baptism was canceled we staid inside my room and he watched me play *Glover* while we listened, on repeat, to *Tee Vee Toons Greatest Hits: Commercials*:

> Here's to good friends
> Tonight is kind of special
> The beer will pour
> Must say something more

Somehow

So tonight

Tonight

Tonight

Let it be Lowenbrau

A week later I would be baptized and I left the church two weeks after that. My mother and stepfather divorced during my sophomore year, after Donna had opened a retail store in Lexington, Chantilly Lane, which later moved to Beavercreek, then Matchmaker International closed in Lexington, then Chantilly Lane closed. After her divorce Donna opened and closed another Matchmaker near Dayton. The Internet had arrived. Melinda had moved to California. My grandmother had died.

Following my high school graduation my mother and I were alone, with nothing but question marks above our futures, living in a two-bedroom apartment on Sally Circle in Centerville, Ohio. I wondered what the fuck I should do in this world, for sincere. I didn't know what I should do, but I had a lot of feeling: The Human Condition, which rests atop The American Dream.

The summer following graduation I spent quiet nights around not much adult world nonsense, my friends and I embracing our dreams through conversations but also, sometimes, feeling it, agreeing that some emotions were wordless, our dreams were in our emotions and it was okay to be quiet because it was great to be around each other. *Definitely*. I'd rather be quiet around a person I want to be around than chatty with a person I feel uncomfortable around, a paranoid adult might say, which perspective I'll develop years after I leave Ohio for places where I'll learn of new people, many people, and more new experiences around more new people will build me toward an emotional place where I didn't ever sit around feeling like I did back when I sat around with my old friends and family in the Midwest.

No one in my life would make me feel as I felt back with my friends and family during my Ohio youth. Shout out to my cousins Sara, Amy, Jenny, my old neighbors William, Robert, Johnny, Jeff, and my old friends Ragavan and Kristi. There was no one else like you for me.

Noted: this stretch of my life was manifested in another way by *My Autobiography Is My Manifesto: Volume One*, an adult-kids novelette hand designed by me, its smaller duplicate titled *automanifest*. Yeah: both those books had been mildly outrageous. I had imprinted an usual feeling upon a book about growing up feeling unusual. Was what I called unusual my imperfection? My imperfections were my own, sure, and I was unusual, yes. That book was both about me and like me, such as my other books written before this one, and this one, based on my understanding that one was able to create one's own dreams, which the country roads of Ohio taught me.

Chapter Three

A perspective I developed while becoming an adult in southern California, a side-story about Portland, Oregon, and a return to the screen dreams of Los Angeles.

Not having realized what life needed from me after I graduated high school, still I believed that my life could lead me toward my dreams. I was such a young adult. What I figured to do was convert my dreams into movies, since movies felt like dreams. After attending two Midwestern universities, then I made plans to move in with my sister and her family in Laguna Beach, California. Melinda by then had three daughters and a husband and what ended up happening was, before I moved to Orange County California my mother did, and I moved into a two-bedroom apartment with her in Laguna Niguel.

In Orange County, in movie classes, I met other people who were roughly my age and felt basically the same about the world as I did. We were all daydreamers who believed the world was magnificent and open. Our dreams felt possible within a world we understood as infinite. Then an Ohio movie friend, following his time in rehab, he moved to California and we signed a year's lease on a one-bedroom apartment. Our beds were inches apart. We attended the same school for the same deeply spiritual reasons, making more friends who were excited to talk about the enormous capabilities of life and movies. While seeing more movies we learned more about movies, as we learned more about people while meeting more people, becoming friends with others who shared our conviction for dreams being capable of becoming lives, and movies being awesome dreams, which felt like the best way to look at things back then.

But it was far easier to turn my thoughts into my dreams than turn my life into my dreams. My reality was not as sweet as my thoughts, and the world explained to me why my dreams weren't within my reach and also, beginning adulthood, I discovered reasons within myself. I was becoming an adult and discovering sometimes that I was not who I wanted to be. What I wanted within me was not always within me. Plus I discovered that social reality was bullshit which must be survived. One must fight for survival within human reality.

And I knew my dream but I didn't know my fight. I knew ordinary life had nothing to do with my dreams. Ordinary life didn't want my dreams. And I didn't want what was ordinary. Though I didn't panic nor give up on life or myself, since that was never helpful. Though sometimes I did that sure.

My first years in California resulted in an existential situation that reached a certain adult complexity which resulted in my daydreams being relocated to Portland, where I lived for two years with a woman whom I treasured. We had both craved those mellow Portland vibes. We cherished weird culture and grassroots culture and like I said we moved to Portland. I hadn't progressed my life situation within the adult world, in terms of my career situation, in terms of personal fulfillment within capitalism, and I hadn't discovered myself as an artist, but I moved northern in a geographical and emotional sense. Happens: how it happens.

I gushed over Portland's industrious self-awareness. It was a city that was proudly aware that one must imagine oneself becoming who one wants to become. Portland had a fabulous bookstore, Powell's Books, which was down the street from our apartment. Downtown. While walking there we would visit EDM (Everyday Music). And on Second and Burnside at Dante's every Wednesday night we would attend Sideshow Speakeasy, which was emceed by William Batty, whom I admired, for being so sensational, for being the emcee to a sideshow of fire breathers, a clown named Bilbo, sword swallowers, et cetera, every Wednesday. Plus, from our apartment on NW 21st Ave., we could walk in another direction to another neighborhood. We could walk down the Alphabet District, where Katherine Dunn lived, and she was my favorite writer, because of a passage in *Geek Love* which became my life motto, a thing said to McGurk, a man with stump legs who admired Arty, a wildly successful sideshow performer, Arty, he had flippers for limbs, it had been his parents' intention for him to be a sideshow performer, Arty, his parents were sideshow performers, and Arty told McGurk about his stumps, "You ought to tan your thighs and walk on them. Wear silver sequin pads and dance on a lit stage where they can see you," since Arty knew that McGurk could conquer his fears through self-confidence, and in my head I often repeat Arty's closing words, "'…you're just going along with what *they* want you to do. *They* want those things hidden away, disguised, forgotten, because they know how much power those stumps could have.'" The writer of that book shopped at the same grocery store where I bought affordable lasagna singles. And there was a movie theater, there were multiple movie theaters in Portland, there were people I became friends with by attending school for movies, and there were friends we had from California, including Brandon, my only book friend I had in my 20s. Me and the treasured woman, we felt we had all we needed at the time, since at the time we needed nothing but life, and life continued to open for us. About her I shall say that she had eyes as big and beautiful as this whole planet.

Through my time in Portland, well into my adulthood then, I persisted in believing, without any evidence, that my life path could lead me toward my dreams. But I couldn't figure out how that would happen, so I began to feel somewhat miserable from a practical perspective. The savings I used to pay my bills, the savings I'd collected during my days working in a tire shop, those savings began to dwindle. I didn't feel against the adult world but I often felt repelled by and not included within it. It would be fine if everything about the normal world stayed the same, since the normal world wanted to be how it was, and I understood, because I felt the same way as an abnormal outsider. What sort of destiny waits for a man like me? My life path was never a single path within the adult world, which was leading me nowhere. I was reminded again, again, again, that who I was was not who the adult world needed. In Portland I stayed on the outside of the adult world, where I felt my dreams and purpose were, which was okay in Portland's opinion, while in most of the adult world people viewed the outside as a cultural wasteland filled with decadence and narcissism. About which I thought: *Okay, trying my best here.* Regardless, as I was saying, my savings were running out. My self-esteem entered a land of fog. I could really not comprehend the adult world. I couldn't for the life of me understand how people survived in the adult world. I just knew there was a price to life, bills to be paid.

My relationship with the treasured woman ended and I moved back to Los Angeles alone. *Back* to Los Angeles. A textual description of the first time the treasured woman and I lived in Brentwood Los Angeles hasn't been mentioned until now. I felt it better for my story to jump ahead to Portland, since I lands back in Los Angeles anyway. There I was in Los Angeles again like I was saying, growing older and still feeling young. Still full of hope, in this city of people filled with hope. Los Angeles: where one's hopes can live. Los Angeles: no promise about your hopes becoming your life. I was now a full adult. And I knew: if one doesn't find one's hopes alive in one's life, one finds something else. This was the nature and logic of self-acceptance, a central component of a Los Angeles personality. One lives however one does. One becomes aware of one's mental afflictions without becoming ruled by them. One finds one's way amid all the others who do the same, and of all the possibilities in life, giving up on oneself is the absolute worst. Some people, when some good is lost from their lives, they interpret this as reason to find more bad, through the dark logic of feeling low and sinking. The bad was always present, yes, and the human condition was choosing to focus on the good or the bad. The essence of The American Dream was a search for the good within your life. Everyone deserved to find goodness in their lives. Human life sounds poetic because reality.

In my life back in Los Angeles, at the age when I should've already become an adult, should've already found success in the adult world (if I ever would), still I reached my hands into my life to grab ahold of my dreams. My bank account had given up on me but I hadn't given up on my dreams. First I worked as a production assistant, then I began to work in the art department. My dreams were bottled inside of movies I still believed, and I desired to crack open my dreams and pour them upon a screen. I moved from Portland back to Los Angeles because Los Angeles was a much larger city and it was where more people made movies, which I wanted to make and had been learning about in Portland (and Orange County). A short movie I wrote and directed, *Motor Away*, played at the Portland International Film Festival. This short had been shot near the Columbia River in an RV owned by the parents of the treasured woman. It was the story of an older male and female couple searching for meaning in their lives. My mother told me that writing *Motor Away* predicted the end of my relationship. Interpretation of that movie was dependent upon the viewer's reaction to the final scene, which was the woman kissing and walking away from the man in the RV. Was she walking away forever? That was for the audience to decide.

The woman in *Motor Away* was played by Gretchen Corbett, an actress most-known from the television show *The Rockford Files*, but within movie land I was glad to have The Girl from *Let's Scare Jessica to Death*. My early California movie friends who lived in Los Angeles still had bright dreams inside their hearts too. They were how I began to be a production assistant. They had traveled to help me make *Motor Away*. They had made a documentary, *Mule Days*, set in Bishop, California. About our possibilities and capabilities for making movies we all felt like Hell Yeah. In Los Angeles we made *Gooses*, which was a short about an Ohioan visiting her sister in Los Angeles. The visiting sister was played by Zena Grey, of *My Soul to Take,* whom the codirector knew through Cinefamily. *Gooses* was a cinematic expression of youthful existence. We were young then (but adults), and we made a short movie with the pop of youth and the energy of cinema, out of adoration, addiction, to life and cinema, feeling proud and excited while making *Gooses*. Our shared life perspective claimed that life was packed full of art—life as a dream was expressed by art, we felt, and we used a cinematic vocabulary to fuse fact and fiction in the creation of our short movie that captured life within that feeling. We felt ourselves becoming professional artists and felt ourselves saying *Here is our voice*. We believed in each other and our voices, our perspectives.

Our emotions were full cans of gas but we couldn't find a car to drive. We almost figured things out but then we didn't.

Now I'll rewind back to when I was attending a university, back in Ohio, living in a dorm with a movie friend whom I've mentioned, and I'm rewinding to further contextualize, mentioning things I've already mentioned and some new things too. My friend and I wanted to study movies, but since our entry into the adult world involved we being young and reckless, first we'd enrolled at a school that didn't have a movie program (we realized upon arriving there). We didn't think much about what school could do in our lives, since we thought so much about how life could feel. What did we want to study in school? Life. Where was life? With our friends. School was a symbol of the adult world, therefore it wanted to organize our lives and thoughts, but we were youngish rebels against the god of organized lives and thoughts. We had a fire in our hearts and we didn't appreciate the world trying to snuff our flames. It's so common it's universal: believing one would rather not live in a world that demands so much but feels so cold. Life can feel lifeless in the adult machine that grinds one's spirit, we felt and discussed along with others, smoking cigarettes upon our dorm stoop at night. My friend and I, we knew each other from high school, and when our friendship began we began shaping our lives into the dream of making movies. Back then there was an American Independent movie scene and we felt that we could be Americans who were businessmen and artists, businessmen who preferred the arts, we wanted to be movie artists. Movies involved a lot of money and we desired to make movies, that was tricky, but we were young and embraced what was tricky. During one early day at Kent State, the first university I attended with my Ohio friend (the second university I attended), while we were under a tree I pointed at the tree and told my friend, "I couldn't write about that tree. What kind of tree is that? I can't begin to describe that leaf, except it's green. And this other stuff, this sidewalk and grass and building, I don't know invigorating words to describe these pedestrian things, which words would but represent the pedestrian invigoration I feel while standing here. Ahhhh—there is the sun setting behind the tree. I'm here with you. You're here with me. This isn't words it's life. Which is why I want to make movies, which can feel alive." I said to my friend, "I want to capture the feeling of being alive now, with a camera," I said and he felt me on that. This perspective guided me through many adult years of my life. Guided by voices. A voice within me guided me back and forward and spun me in a circle. The last script I wrote was titled *Gem City*. Gem City was a nickname for Dayton Ohio, where the whole movie would take place, except for a short trip to Los Angeles in the middle, which trip had been the basis for *Gooses*. I wrote *Gem City* with a California movie friend who once called me his soulmate but stopped engaging me after we couldn't find the road toward making *Gem City*. My life was a reality not a movie. My California movie friends found their own career paths, one establishing himself as a cinematographer, one becoming an editor, one composing music scores, and I gave up on movies. As far as I could tell, the movie world wasn't for me. I wasn't a fan. I wanted something besides a three-act structure. I wanted explosive narrative textures and I wanted to imagine from a perspective which I couldn't find in movies but found in my life.

My life felt to me far more spacious than the parochial narratives of most movies, and since I couldn't find a way to become a successful artistic writer/director, even with people believing in me and wanting the same thing I couldn't find more than my friends and family who would believe in my perspective of cinema. I would look away from cinema though stayed in my thoughts, a camera remained to me a symbol of a mind, and my mind as a camera what I did was I pointed myself back at pure words not meant for a screen, beginning to see a page as a stage and words as actors. Now for me cinema took place in words, and I made movies in books, continuing to move forward however I did as I did, chasing the heels of my dreams, always. My dream wasn't to do what the world asked me to do, my dream was to follow the desires of my soul. Though my soul wasn't composed of words, my soul was amorphous, like all souls, and what I did was I searched for its patterns, the same as I searched for patterns in life. Trying to save my soul. What my soul believed was *Words will never betray you.* Only sometimes I betrayed words, such as when I chose movies over them, but I didn't first choose to be a director, my initial plan had been to become a screenwriter. While writing scripts in Brentwood, Los Angeles I walked across San Vicente Boulevard with *Catcher in the Rye.* I was always a reader. I was always thinking of writing. The suicide of David Foster Wallace was tragic to me, as it was tragic to all literary types back then. In Los Angeles I watched more movies than I ever had before, watched them in a more serious way than I ever had before, but still watching movies didn't make me feel as deeply about the world—movies didn't seem to puncture my sense of life—-as much as reading books. Werner Herzog came close to digging inside of me, but how I felt during *Stroszek* was what Saul Bass described in *Herzog.* In a movie theater I would feel excited, but within a bookstore I would feel wondrous; and excitement is an emotional path, while wonder is a path toward knowledge. So feeling both excited and wondrous was best, I felt while growing up. The energy contained by the words held within books—the same energy I found within myself and life—this magnetized me from my youth, instigating my imaginative faculties and leading me toward creative endeavors, leading me toward beginning to write a book as a young boy, and writing movie scripts as a young adult. The first book I began to write, as a boy, was about a boy, pulled inside the land of television, by a monster. The first movie scripts I wrote were shorts for my Ohio friend to direct, such as: *Day-Glo*; *Everything's Fine, Thanks; Holy Shit; Yesterday Is Tomorrow*. Together we once began to make a short horror triptych, one I titled *Yellow-Jacket Brain Fever* a.k.a. *I Love That You Love Me*. The first feature length script I wrote wasn't *Gem City*, that wasn't even the first script I'd written with that California friend (*Examples of Apple Food*, a moody metaphysical blue-collar crime caper), but the *Gem City* script became an ending to my writing with that friend, and an ending to me writing scripts. Like I mentioned in another way with other words, I hadn't turned my eyes away from books because of words, it had been a personal reason, so what I did was I turned my eyes away from movies and back toward books, words meant to be words, pure words, having through my life chased after words as much as dreams.

I held true love for words, adored them, treasured them, learned of them by listening to them. I listened to the words I heard and read, and one becomes what one adores, so I began to wonder of the writerly type I would become.

My childish aspirations strangled my adult world necessities, in terms of the adult world not caring about me as a writer, no one paying me to be a writer, and I was only growing older.

The world was ready to give up on me but I wasn't ready to give up on my myself: I felt satisfaction being suffocated by my dreams. All things happen: how they happen. I happened: how I happened. Life wasn't easy and my reality never mirrored my dreams, but what ended up happening was my dreams became my reality, actually, since the outsiders and outcasts and loner rebels were my favorites and always the ones to whom I could relate. I became what I adored as one does like I already said. Did I ever adore the lives which looked easy? No I didn't. Did I ever adore the outsiders who *brought it*? That's what I'm saying. My favorite people were the ones who changed the temperature of the room once they entered, they were my favorites, especially the ones so weighed down by life that they could barely stand anything, those people made total sense to me. It was pure logic that the heaviness of reality would drag one down, I believed. People who felt the same were my favorite people. I never wanted to be with the popular, I wanted to be with the irregular. I never wanted to lead the world to a better place, I wanted to be with the world toward a funky place. I hadn't wanted adult happiness as a child, I'd wanted reality, all of it.

Chapter Four

A mirror of words and here I am.

In my adult years I found myself a strange creature who was not management material, and I couldn't find my way to give two fucks about the adult world, which assisted the adult world in giving no fucks about me.

Everything felt perfectly fucked but I was getting used to it. I was getting used to being myself, well past the age of becoming an adult, still not successful within the adult world, though movies and books remained inside of me, those my dream shapes like I've been saying, this all happened because of my soul. After *Gem City* expired I then began to publish books with another California friend, Morgan. He coined the name: Neon Burrito Publishing. We decided to publish the third book of poems we'd written: *Eudaimonia*. Then we published our other two. Then we published all three in a collection: *Basic Mutant Psychosis*. And after *Gem City* had been written I had begun writing my autofiction novella *Larry Angeles*, the results of which I hadn't known, but which I then published.

I have heard it said that books are for the working class, and it may not be only for them, but it most certainly is for them, and I wrote a book from within it, wracked with common existential and material diseases, seeking bliss within the sacred purity of philosophy. I wrote a novella as a disillusioned person clinging to reality as if falling from a cliff, screaming as I was slipping of the horrors that I could be seeing, which was also the type of writing I enjoyed reading.

Was I person chosen to become a writer? No. I hadn't been chosen to become a writer, I'd chosen to become a writer. I wasn't a gift of creation, creation was a gift to me, which I'd realized as a child. The difficulty in not being a gift of creation had been addressed and readdressed by me throughout my life. Why did my days go on, why did I go on—why I lived and wrote was because I lived to write, the answer is in the question. And this made me feel small in a big world, but that was preferable to feeling big in a small mind.

My most-recent previous book, *Oscar Wilde's The Picture of Dorian Gray*, attempted to create a narrative which illustrated my personal dimensions of life-acquired philosophy, while actively engaging the reader as a companion. That was the main narrative, though the book included two fragments plus an adult-kids book (with illustrations by Morgan). The additional material had been included since the main text mentioned it, and as a reader whenever I heard a writer speak of recent abandoned projects I would think, "Let me see them." So I showed mine. That was literary oversharing and maybe that was tacky but I've heard of worse. A reader has interpreted *Oscar Wilde's The Picture of Dorian Gray* as me feeling lost and confused about myself, though I myself didn't feel that was the case. I sought not myself but my possibility.

Sometimes often times on regular occasions I felt not lost and confused inside of myself, but lost and confused inside this world. What I wanted of myself I knew, I continued searching for it, but I didn't know what this world wanted of me, didn't know how to search for it. I searched for my entry point into the adult world filled with all its possibilities, wondering what my possibility was, writing of my search.

Chapter Five

A spectrum of recent life occurrences.

On July 4th, 2017, in Los Angeles, California, USA, there was a lightning-strike of a president and I was reading Kerouac's *The Subterraneans* while beginning to write this book. That night my feet cruised Oakwood toward The New Beverly for *Okja*, and later I fell asleep while watching *The Crow* from my futon. Yup, that was an adult day I lived within other people's dreams.

My life was standard human stuff. Not too many problems, except the monotonous frustrations of the adult world, and the occasional problem of dark flowers blooming inside of me. Nothing unique about me, which, through the mostly-cruel logic of social psychology, this very fact, of so many people being exactly like me, throughout history, speakers of dreams, there being so many people like me neither helped me be myself nor helped others believe that I mattered. *One of many.* I tended to relate with all these people who were common and welcome as writers but uncommon and unwelcome in the adult world. Simply: a writer wasn't necessary within the adult world. No one began a business meeting with, "We're going to discuss Ernest Becker's *The Denial of Death*, 'Human Character as a Vital Lie", part one chapter four." No one ended a business meeting with, "Make sure for next week you read up to 'The Spell Cast by Persons—The Nexus of Unfreedom', part two chapter seven." In Los Angeles I wasn't alone being alone, trapped in my dreams. Meeting others often meant experiencing the static electricity of city dreams. Many other people would radiate their own dreams they were trapped inside, just like me. But different dreams, often. I met plenty of actors. I wanted not to be an actor, I wanted to be the furthest away from being an actor a person could be. And on occasion around some people I would think that Los Angeles craved not humanity but its reflection; other people could make me feel more alone, for their dreams would cause them to see the world much differently than I did. My dream involved conquering not a struggle for success but a struggle for life. Through time and experience I learned my life disaster was my own, my perspective was my own, and another person's life and perspective were their own. That was how things were, everyone was living their own lives, and I tried never to hold it against a person for being themselves. Based on the particulars of myself and others, there was a statistical unlikelihood that I would often encounter others like me, given all the numbers of ways there were to be a person, all the infinite possibilities within finite lives. People like me seem to want to meet people different than the people we meet. We seem to want to be people other than the people we are. I wanted there to be another world where my soul stuff would be the same soul stuff of the world, yet this was not the world I lived within.

Then it was another nighttime in July and I was on a street corner smoking a cigarette alone, exactly like thousands of other lonely people. So I was a normal loner weirdo and that didn't bother me when I didn't think about it—being weird was like aging, you see a different world, you know you do that's just how it is, how it has been and how it will be. It's not easy but a full life was worth it. I was myself and that was outrageous I agree, I was ridiculous I concede.

The next morning I awoke wrapped not in wishes but in hope. I lied suspended in satisfaction upon my futon, without feelings related to my unknowable day.

It felt good to be alive when all I felt was alive. Yet of course I knew that when I rose from my futon I would confront the reality of my day, which would not be made of my desires. What would make my day? Reality. At best I could be a co-presenter. Before I rose from my futon I took out my phone and checked the various things one checks on their phone, such as the Internet, and what friends were social sharing. I would imagine my days based on emotional suggestions by friends and news. Sometimes I heard awful things in the news, and I would think, "Okay, time to help the world become better." Sometimes I would hear the wonderful news of others and I would think, "Great, keep going." Sometimes I would become involved in Internet discussions which turned out to be helpful or not. "I don't understand why you don't like Budd Boetticher." That day I found nothing on the Internet, though I searched for a couple of hours, switching between my computer and phone. The materials for my day I couldn't find, so I'd go to find the materials myself. This was how I often began my days: searching for my feelings. For hours. Before my day began. Before nighttime, when they would waiting there for me.

Sometimes in a day I wouldn't find my feelings, sometimes I would find them and lose them again. During my days off from work, now and then I would return to lie upon my futon, and I wouldn't always nap but I would lie there with my eyes closed, waiting for my thoughts to settle. My swirling thoughts could lead me anywhere, and my settled thoughts would bring me toward one place or another. This I knew from experience being myself.

A description of the swirl: thoughts of anything/everything, all my awareness of reality, liquid memories, liquid concepts, with special interest on the parts of reality I was unaware of but had recently heard about, and speculation regarding many things I might not know. The swirl often represented the perpetual emergency life felt like to me, which pushed me toward internal exile. Reading books brought me the swirl. Reading Wikipedia articles brought me the swirl. The swirl developed while I wrote, for example after I wrote a line which instigated prolonged and meaningful reflection. I would lie on my futon with my eyes closed until my thoughts settled, with caffeine pounding in my chest, and many times I'd dance my feet across Mid-City West sidewalks. An open sky could release the swirl from me, especially the night sky—the sun of Los Angeles was both a treasure and a bit much. I was a person of pale skin who worried of skin damage, wrinkles, sunburns, and cancer. I didn't always remember to understand the importance of sunscreen and/or install it, I preferred to walk the city at night.

Within my swirl I searched for the concrete. A swirl of thoughts began as such: "I'm curious how we'd all act if humans were immortal." A concrete stance: "It's Tuesday and I have to do my laundry." Swirl: "I haven't the time to become who other people want me to become, since I spend much of my time working on becoming myself." Concrete: "I should trim my fingernails." Swirl: "What are my feelings regarding being alive?" Concrete: "I will go write."

Sometimes I would lie down, but I would be on my futon most of my free time at any rate. Writing or reading when I wasn't walking, I'd rest on my futon which faced blue draped windows, a foot of mine wiggling, or my thighs shaking sometimes, always just in my undies, lying on my futon writing. Unless my roommate was away, then sometimes I would sit and write upon the living room recliner, in front of a window which faced the back of Canter's Deli and Fairfax Avenue. Depending upon the day's weather condition, and likely, a fan would be on in one room or the other. Sometimes, if he was away at the time, I paced the hallway of the two-bedroom apartment where I lived with Brett Buckalew. Always: music played from the computer I wrote upon. I would only turn off music if instead of writing I was reading. I would keep music on if I was inside a swirl. Music was ideal for a swirl. *The problem with reality was a lack of background music.* The me of my past would have daily watched a movie or three—I was not that same person then, when my thoughts looked away from the idea of making movies. Only on occasion would I go to theaters or watch movies in my room.

The condition of men eating alone at cheap food places, especially diners, but actually everywhere with cheap food, I was aware of it, because I was part of it. How many times had I sat alone in a room populated by other companionless men? Many times. We men could become a lonely crowd in public places. To others we could look quite sad, but to ourselves we were fighting out our days through the strength we found. Our strength to go outside, for someone else to make our food... A common occurrence during these days was me eating at Jack in the Box, my least-favorite fast food restaurant. And fast food was well-known as a general bad idea. I had agreed about that for so long. This place, such a bad idea, had been calling me back these days. The Jack in the Box down Fairfax, under 3rd Street. I would eat at it on Saturday nights, typically with other single men at their own tables. The gloom within the room felt real to me, and perhaps it wasn't gloom at all. Was it only a bother to see us? We were polite. We were considerate of others. We were quiet. We were alone. Jack in the Box accepted EBT, cards issued through Temporary Assistance to

Needy Families. People who would call themselves respectable wouldn't and didn't eat here, which was why I ate here, for the people who wouldn't worry about their respectability were always, to me, filled with the most life. Respectability I saw as one of those social illusions humans create, and I was against every social mask that fostered a social hierarchy creating perspectives upon which people viewed themselves as superior to others. The only looks I tapped into were real or rebel, and one would see a rebel or two at Jack in the Box for sure. Because it was such a bad idea. Always: fuck it.

What kind of person was I? In terms of being political I was egalitarian, which isn't a political word. I looked for when the right got along with the left and vice versa. All the ways to look at life, I preferred to look in front of me, for example at Jack in the Box under 3rd Street, Mid-City West, on a Saturday night. A solid allegory of melodramatic value would be to say that my life itself was a meal from a fast food restaurant, and I was a fan of melodrama. I was a fan of emotions like I could even. One particular Saturday night I was at this Jack in the Box for a delightful item named the H'angry Chicken Hash. It was composed of five nuggets, two hash browns, with bbq and ranch sauce. One ate it with a fork.

Plus I bought the cheapest burger, without pickles. And I ordered a medium-sized Oreo milkshake, which I'd drink with two of their narrow straws. Was this not how they ate in Rome? When I sat, to my left was a homeless lady with camo pants. Blue plastic bags in her hands. To my right was a clean man with long hair and a long beard. He wore a clean white t-shirt underneath a clean gray Chicago Bulls tank top. He had a finger pointed at a page and he spoke aloud and laughed while he read a book. I was reading from *The Notebooks of Malte Laurids Brigge*. I didn't know what the other man was reading from, and I cherished the wonder he gave me. I strongly believed in every laugh he made. I heard, "Order 322." I heard, "Right here." A lady entered to sit and talk on her phone. Then the man with the long hair and long beard put on a clean blue baseball hat, getting ready to leave. This was beyond charming to me: he placed his book in a plastic bag. I used two straws to scoop whip cream from the bottom of my Oreo milkshake cup before I left shortly after him. They were speaking Spanish in the kitchen but I heard "McGregor" and realized it was the night of the boxing match (August 26). Outside I saw the clean man with the long hair, long beard. He was adjusting his shopping cart parked at the side of Jack in the Box. I didn't know his life but I knew he spoke aloud and laughed while he read, and he placed his book inside a plastic bag. Then I looked at my phone to check the results of the boxing match, but it hadn't started yet.

The place of my employment at the time of this writing I would not write of as if it invented problems new to the human race. There were lousy situations which occurred between myself and others, but another person could be a perpetuator as well as I could. There was the reality of me being at a job, there was the reality me doing my job, there was the reality of my job being at a corporate-owned bookstore. It was a corporate retail job and the best of its kind in terms of jobs my coworkers and I could imagine ourselves having. I was the lowest rung and I had been there for almost four years. I was a bookseller. There was business and there was personal. I was paid minimum wage and given part-time hours. It was from a lack of pay and respect that I had been meaning to escape from there for some time, as discussed in *Larry Angeles, Cosmic Robotics*, and *Oscar Wilde's The Picture of Dorian Gray.*

Another day I was in an office at the place where I worked, and a manager was telling me, as a friend, that I would never be promoted within the company. She noted that three other coworkers had mentioned they would rather not work with me. That was some supreme shittalking from some supreme shittalkers. I mentioned "I'd rather not work with anyone, but I do." The previous day I had asked the scheduling manger why I was receiving fewer hours. The next day the store manager and the scheduling manager confirmed what the other manager had told me, that I would never be promoted within the company, owing to my metrics. I questioned how my metrics were being counted and proposed myself as a good worker, which I felt I was. In a loud, stern voice the store manager explained I could have a more positive attitude. I commented that I didn't complain to my managers about my coworkers. The store manager said my coworkers had been asked about their feelings. I mentioned that no one asked about my feelings while she was already speaking to me from her business perspective which I knew I was in the room to listen to. I was ready to listen to the things I should do to be better at my job, how I should be nicer, sell more things, make the customers glad to spend money. The store manager was doing her job and from that perspective I didn't think she was being unreasonable. She went on about policies and when she concluded I mentioned, "I'm 33." I couldn't understand why the room seemed against me but they said they weren't. And they said they couldn't give me a continuous number of weekly hours or imagine promoting me, mentioning only potential hope for the future. This meeting occurred after I had a recent job interview somewhere else. I hadn't gotten the new job yet so I remained composed. I was able to remain composed. I knew I had to leave this bookseller job in this corporate book store. Again I mentioned my positive attributes. There was some laughter related to some other things said without being mentioned, laughter felt nice, at a certain point all we wanted was to be out of the manager's office and doing other things. When the meeting ended I felt sure that I *needed* to leave this job. This felt clear to me, though I wished it had been clear to me that the people I worked with cared about me and my future. Was I hopeless, was I impossible? Simply: I wasn't worth the effort from a business perspective.

I was an alien who crash landed on adult planet. July had become August and then it was the end of September when I had finished reading *I Love Dick* by Chris Kraus, which I once started without finishing.

> She was an American artist, and for the first time it
> occurred to her that perhaps the only thing she had to offer
> was her specificity. By writing Dick she was offering her
> life as Case Study.

I couldn't continue writing *Stormy Fortune* while I was reading *I Love Dick* because I was convinced that I needed to finish *I Love Dick* before I could ever write again. I thought that was me being practical. From July to September I read as if the reading bug had bit me, which it had. I sometimes lose my reading fever, but I always get bit again. I got the new job, which I would start mid-October. The new job was related to books as my previous job had been, but it was related in a more direct, meaningful way. I was ready to leave my old job and begin my new one, and I knew I had fears, but I knew that I had more ahead of me than just my fears.

Chapter Six

Descriptions of reading as a foundational element within my life experience.

During July, August, and September, I spent much of my time reading not writing. Hardly any writing, except for this book I began to structure through notes I made on my phone while walking, establishing the book outline. Mainly I experienced a reading frenzy, based on how wonderful reading can make me feel: in terms of wanting to write, how close I can feel with other writers; in terms of wanting to read, how close I can feel with other readers!

The more I learned of books and writing the more I learned of how much there was to learn. When I experienced lusty reading fits I read as much as I could whenever I could. I had books on my phone, in order to have something to read at any time. A classic phone book of mine was Fernando Pessoa's *The Book of Disquiet*. "Life is whatever we make it. The traveller is the journey. What we see is not what we see but who we are." I had that always and could read it while eating a burrito. Through my life I was delighted by travels I took through the massive, timeless land of words. Mostly I read books not on my phone but in their physical form, since I liked the physical feeling of pages behind me, pages ahead of me.

How *The Love of Books* came to be published under The Barnes & Noble Library of Essential Reading I'm not sure, but I'm sure I bought and read Richard de Bury's book. The title *Story Fortune* is from a line in it:

Books delight us, when prosperity smiles upon us; they comfort us inseparably when stormy fortune frowns upon us.

I felt like Richard de Bury understood the power of words, which he ascribed to being from God. Chapter Nine was titled "How, Although We Preferred the Works of the Ancients, We Have Not Condemned the Studies of the Moderns". In this chapter he wrote of books as a historic school of philosophy. He lamented the sad times he lived within, during which "there is none who begins to take place as a new author." This was written in the fourteenth century by a bishop and royal counselor who desired to extol the virtues of books, initiating librarianship.

Would Richard de Bury have wanted to read me? May it at least be that he would have wanted to collect me, as a bibliophile. His book was known as *The Philobiblon* and there he was, all the way back then, forming visions about the colossal tapestry known as writing. One has so much life, and so little time to read all there is to read.

Shihāb al-Dīn Ahmad ibn 'Abd al-Wahhāb al-Nuwayrī felt the same way back in the fourteenth century, and I read from the Penguin Classics edition of his *The Ultimate Ambition in the Arts of Erudition*. Shihāb al-Dīn al-Nuwayrī had composed what was considered a type of encyclopedia, back before encyclopedias. I read from book two, chapter four, "On the Ruler, His Subjects, And Advisers; and on the Craft of Secretaryship", since I was interested in what he considered the best things to mention about becoming a writer. I read the sections titled "On Writing and the Different Kinds of Scribes", "On the Description of the Scribe and What He Must Know", and "On the General Knowledge of the Scribe".

Shihāb al-Dīn al-Nuwayrī made it very clear that a writer should be a massive fucking reader, and that anyone who wanted to write in the future should know what had been written in the past:

> If he does not do so, let him know that he will find himself in one valley, while the craft of secretaryship will be in another.

From the Harvard University Press edition of Dante Alighieri's *La Vita Nuova*, the beginning of Chapter XVI:

> After I'd written that, I realized there was more to say, and I was prompted to write another in which I could say four things I hadn't said yet.

The narrator then explains the four things his next sonnet will describe. I appreciated: the narrator's oversharing; how Dante Alighieri wrote in the vernacular; how he wrote as a human. To me it seemed that much of writing was about forming a reasonable framework for descriptions of being human. In terms of emotions and a human perspective, I felt a direct link between myself and *La Vita* Nuova, not from having lived that life but from having read stories of a similar nature. I knew the feeling. The explanatory summaries made before sonnets within *La Vita Nuova* inspired the short explanations before chapters in *Stormy Fortune.*

La Vita Nuova was written at the end of the thirteenth century, in the time of the codex, which had replaced the scroll in the sixth century of a Greco-Roman world. A codex written manuscript. After the time of *La Vita Nuova* a Late Manuscript Culture evolveed, during which time there arrived tables of contents, chapter lists, colophons, and page numbers in Arabic numerals. Johannes Gutenberg's fifteenth-century invention of the printing press changed the game. His invention made the game, and from there evolved the idea of a novel.

The sixteenth-century writer of the novella *Lazarillo de Tormes* was Anonymous, although all signs point toward the writer being a reader, back in the youth of novels existing. *Lazarillo de Tormes* had been the literary introduction of a genre which became known as picaresque, with a pícaro main character who was "a product of his environment, often anti-social, sometimes delinquent, and a literary anti-hero." It arrived within the Spanish Golden Age and was written "…in a style which uses the ordinary prose of life, rather than in an artificial and prescribed literary manner," as Michael Alpert mentioned in his opening notes to the Penguin Classics edition. The opening paragraph of Chapter 6 is an example of what astonished me:

After this I lived with an artist who painted tambourines for a living. My job was to mix his colors for him and the life was very hard.

There was a vibrant sensation of life perspective within the storytelling of *Lazarillo de Tormes*, which delighted me, and I was able to relate to this character written so long ago. His life path was a continuous flight forward, a constant quest toward another day.

"Oh, God, from whom nothing is hidden but everything revealed; to whom nothing is impossible but all things possible."

By the time Charles Baudelaire was around, in the nineteenth century, novels had *been round*, and he wondered where they were headed. He explored the capabilities of writing in a modern world. He in fact established the term "modernity" and defined its features of ephemerality. In prose-poetry he wrote of what it felt like to be alive then. Charles Baudelaire impacted me, hit me hard. For example, within *Paris Spleen*, his book of prose poems, in "Widows" he described poets and philosophers who "love to direct their avid speculations" upon what is "feeble, destitute, orphaned, and forlorn." From the Melville House collection The Art of the Novella, I read the only novella Charles Baudelaire wrote, *Fanfarlo*. His writing further expanded my concept of human dimensions capable of being conveyed through words and stories.

The protagonist of *Fanfarlo*, Samuel, first encounters in a public park the woman Madame de Cosmelly, who at the time was reading a novel by Walter Scott. Elated by finding her reading, Samuel first criticizes Walter Scott as being boring, then he offers to share with Madame de Cosmelly his own writing:

> "Madame," Samuel said sententiously, "in the nineteenth century the true public is women; your approval will make me greater than twenty academies."

When they see each other later, Madame de Cosmelly tells him:

> "Monsier, I am only a woman, and, consequently, my judgment does not count for much; but I find that the sorrows and love affairs of gentlemen authors hardly resemble the sorrows and love affairs of other men."

Samuel replies by saying, "Madame, pity me, or rather pity yourself...", and what follows is absolute mansplaining. A brilliant illustration of the male ego. After pages and pages of Samuel mansplaining, then Madame de Cosmelly is able to reply, starting by saying:

"I understand, Monsieur, everything that a soul can suffer as a result of that loneliness, and how a heartfelt ambition such as yours must be devoured so quickly in its solitude; but your sorrows, which are yours alone, as far I can untangle from your pompous words, come from weird needs that remain unsatisfied and almost possible to satisfy."

Calling it. From here Fanfarlo is revealed to be an actress whom the husband of Madame de Cosmelly has fondness for, so Samuel promises to intercede, then he develops a fondness for Fanfarlo, so they marry, and Madame de Cosmelly thanks Samuel after she reunites with her husband. The book then gives a quick description of Samuel and Fanfarlo living realities founded on personal illusions.

The myriad ways people imagined themselves developed alongside the myriad ways people imagined books. Both *Fanfarlo* and *La Vita Nuova* were said to be based on stories from the lives of their writers. After having dipped my toes into the past, then I felt the need to swim within the present. I dove inside *Bluets*, by Maggie Nelson, whom I had come to admire through *The Argonauts*. One can read contemporary literature to know of quests taking place inside the land of words. Maggie Nelson was an aspect within what was sometimes called The Golden Age of Nonfiction. Maggie Nelson was an aspect of feminism. I would say that I hoped feminism was for everybody and The Golden Age of Nonfiction too. In that time nonfiction writing was being appreciated again, and fresh human perspectives were finding illumination within the land of words, which I cherished. How could a reader who liked to know the writer behind the writing not like nonfiction? I was destined to like this type of writing, and I enjoyed contemporary literary perspectives. I liked best the writers who were readers. Maggie Nelson was a reader and her words provided me with utter transparency in regard to her as a person. While *The Argonauts* existed within a more traditional book narrative form, *Bluets* had numbered sections and was wild with its form, but continuous with its wmotions. At section 75 she wrote, "Mostly I have felt myself becoming a servant of sadness. I am still looking for beauty in that." This was section 229:

> Cornell's diary entry for February 28, 1947: "Resolve this day as before to transcend in my work the overwhelming sense of sadness that has been so binding and wasteful in past."

I was delighted to follow along with the emotional textures of *Bluets*, and I admired the nimble perspectives of Maggie Nelson, the poetic interconnectivity of her narrative about a person at a certain time in her life. She continued to be an inspiration to me.

So I decided to read more of that type of book, and since *Bluets* was published by Wave Books I read another book from them, Renee Gladman's *Calamities*. Within it she described her writing process:

> As I had done before, I would make the way the book changed me a book in itself, or at least make an essay that would draw a picture of the story.

Writes who are readers, I treasured them; I adored *Calamities*.

My reading fever also lead me into a first time reading of Dennis Johnson's *Jesus' Son*, Kurt Vonnegut's *A Man Without a Country*, and *On the Move* by Oliver Sacks, *The Face: A Time Code* by Ruth Ozeki, *Conversations* by César Aira, *The Sarah Book* by Scott McClanahan, plus Mori Ōgain's *The Wild Geese* (which had been loaned to me by a coworker reading Japanese classics to become familiar with his wife's culture), plus-plus I started over and finished another book I'd once begun, *Spurious* by Lars Iyer, in addition to the books mentioned in the previous chapter, and some children's books I'm not listing. Each book further expanded my concept of possibility within books and words and humans. I listed the array because each one in some way or another became a part of this book, what I read and live leading me toward what I write, *Stormy Fortune*. The main components of writing upon my mind at the time have been mentioned, the summary being that I believed people and books experience parallel life growth, as Oliver Sacks referenced (quoting his friend: "Every perspective is an act of creation"), and books have been like this through human history, as Richard de Bury and Shihāb al-Dīn al-Nuwayrī mentioned.

Chapter Seven

My relation to Murphy's Law.

To rewind: I was an aspect of my life worries, which worried me. About myself I used to think at the beginning of each day: "Brought back from the dead again. Why?"

Back then each day I had to find the reason I was brought back from the dead *again*, that was my regular morning feeling, and the reasons weren't always easy to find. I wrote from inside myself back then, as now. As far as I could tell I was a man whose emotions thought out loud. I was of a metaphysical, casual intensity. Stable emotional severity. Existential basic stuff. As a future adult I may let go of myself enough that I will be able to see myself in the world with further clarity, and then I might either continue searching inside myself or begin writing narratives more story driven, but for me back then my life was a mystery and I wrote of it as such.

It was not as if I felt like my greatness was bound to happen. Every day I began my day by trying to find a rock solid reason not to worry about my personal problems. Problems: always around. Always. But I attempted to throw planks upon pits of misery and walk across them as if without a problem beneath me, when I could do that. What I knew was worrying never helped. But there was a dark garden within my soul since birth, and on occasion I didn't make the best life decisions. On occasion I made bullshit decisions.

What calmed me during reflections upon my past bad decisions was perspective on how many humans there were who made bad decisions. All humans made bad decisions. I didn't think I made the worst decisions. I speculated that I made terrible choices in terms of business, since I couldn't develop a business perspective, but mostly I just made regular terrible human choices of a casual, passionate variety, based on the world around me and who I was.

Terrible choices: I'd made some. This world: hadn't kissed my fate or fortune. The path I took toward making myself a writer was similar to what I was saying earlier about throwing planks upon my pit of misery while living, each word here a plank over a pit within me. And, remembering how many humans make bad choices, in different ways, on a day in July what settled my nerves was an adage known as Murphy's law: *Anything that can go wrong will go wrong.*

This adage helped me feel better owing to its general philosophy, which reminded me that one works past what could go wrong, and the person who coined Murphy's Law, Edward Murphy, had been an R&D Officer at the Wright Field Aircraft Lab. He'd been referring to another person's wrongness when he said it. I visited Wright Patterson Air Force Base when I was younger, with my stepfather when he worked on weekends. Edward Murphy worked on testing high-speed rocket sleds. In a cosmic sense I was like Kevin Bacon in regard to his phrase, only a few degrees separate, and therefore through my accurate sense of phantom patterns I could tell that Murphy's Law would be stamped within my life, always there, always true. Still: get the high-speed rocket sled to work.

In the United Kingdom there's Sod's law, adapted from Finagle's law of dynamic negatives: *Anything that can go wrong, will—at the worst possible moment.* Murphy's Law was from Ohio and that was something. What kind of thing was that? Some. I didn't worry much about it while I wrote or lived, but the entire time I thought it true as hell. Terrible choices like I said I'd made them, things had gone wrong, I'd gone wrong, which fact I tried not to dwell upon. The worst I'd done had lead me to who I was, and was I the worst, no, there was worse (life circumstance). I would make terrible choices again as long as I lived, I guessed. I'd work on my life until I died. Not dead yet.

Chapter Eight

Sincere movie time.

L.I.E. came out in 2001 and starred young Paul Dano in a relationship with middle-aged Brian Cox. I thought it was both a devastating portrait of reality and a fantastic movie. It was like a suburban version of Larry Clark's *Kids*. It captured dimensions of a hard and bittersweet life. After I saw it, after it was released on DVD, then I considered it a fresh, riveting, cinematic representation of humans living in emotional swamplands. Growing up, emotional, I felt as if I lived within a swampland too.

Becoming an adult I became tired of what had begun to tire me in my youth, how movies were such fucking movies, total bullshit, and I could suspend my disbelief or I could drop my jaw and watch life inside a movie. I did the former and I practiced the latter. Most every extraordinary movie I saw back then I saw by DVD, before I lived in Los Angeles, before Blu-ray, after VHS. *Trees Lounge* came out in 1996, was written/directed by Steve Buscemi (who was such an icon of reality to me), he also starred, and within the bleak context of depressing alcoholism he depicted resilient black humor. One could *feel it.* That was the type of movie which I felt the world needed. I needed *Trees Lounge*, I felt, when I watched it in my friend's Ohio basement, with some other friends, on a Saturday night when we were youngish.

Noi the Albino was a true dear friend of ours. His quiet life reminded us of ours. My friends and I felt as if we'd been with the people of *Gummo,* our fondness coming from *Gummo* being set in Ohio, and feeling like some parts of Ohio sometimes. Here was a thing about cartoons: if you're going to suspend disbelief, suspend all of it. We'd dream ourselves into *Night on the Galactic Railroad, Spirited Away* and dream within the romantic realities of *Live Flesh, Il Postino.* We were Midwestern people who adored fantastic movies about ordinary people. And we felt that some of the best and worst aspects of people could be portrayed through movies. Movies were kaleidoscopic visions of reality, which cinematic quality cinematic people liked to mention: *Kaleidoscopic*. My friends and I were passionate about movies, so we admired passionate filmmakers who made passionate movies, contemporary classics like *Friday* and *Rushmore*, classic classics like *L'Avventura* and *Seven Samurai*. Movies were people wrapped in movie dreams and we felt them on that. We wanted to make something like *El Mariachi*, but the action would be emotions. That was on our minds and seemed within our reach during our late teenage years.

Then I grew older, because of biology, and developing an idea to make a movie motivated me to develop my idea about movies. I dove inside the concept of movies from a high board. A quality I valued was movies being flower petals on a path of space and time. As an adult I told people that my favorite Hollywood movies were from 1927-33 and that was true. There had been Charlie Chaplin, Mary Pickford, Erich von Stroheim, D.W. Griffith, and others who helped Hollywood become what I'm about to get to, my favorite time period in Hollywood cinema, 1927-1933.

What I've heard is that viewers were rattled by *Frankenstein* as much as people are capable of being rattled. All the many years later and everyone still wanted to make a movie that captured the full reality portrayed in Tod Browning's *Freaks—*

but either a person wanted to be like Tod Browning or a person was equal to Tod Browning, in terms of how could one become better? Same thing for Clara Bow, who was titled *It*, after all. What was the first movie to use a boom pole? Clara Bow's first talkie, directed by Dorothy Arzner. Though my favorite Dorothy Azner movie was *Merrily We Go to Hell*. My favorite Barbara Stanwyck movie was *Night Nurses*. The Norma Shearer movie *The Divorcee* portrayed the essence of some real shit, I felt. Mae West, "Why don't you come up some time, and see me." The dynamic force of Paul Robeson as *The Emperor Jones*. The utterly absurd strength of James Cagney in *Lady Killer*, developed after *The Public Enemy* had established him as a movie gangster. Paul Muni in *Scarface*— Paul Muni in *I Am a Fugitive from a Chain Gang*! And I wondered: what movie could feel more joyful than *The Smiling Lieutenant*, besides perhaps *Love Me Tonight*... what movies had the emotional rhythms of Murnau, his *Sunrise: A Song of Two Humans* and *City Girl*. Cherry on top: my belief was Josef von Sternberg's *The Docks of New York* used cinema to paint the people of a city as well as cinema could. Its cinematic genre was named city operas.

Popular ideas about how to think of movies shifted while my adult life began, but I had unglued myself from the patterns of contemporary popular movies and jumped into the century-plus years of global cinema because that was possible. Plus life gave me a bonus, for people my age also felt like movies should feel like reality, so young people began to make movies that felt like life felt to them. *Funny Ha Ha, The Puffy Chair, Goodbye Solo, Quiet City, The GoodTimes Kid, Hannah Takes The Stairs, Frownland, The Pleasures of Being Robbed, William Never Married, Snow on Tha Bluff, Bad Fever—* movies which felt made by people, movies about people who acted like people, this was a favorite type of movie of mine, like I keep saying. Where did I discover the most outrageous? Suspension of disbelief movies. Which movies made me feel the most alive? People movies.

I wasn't a person with heroes, I desired all of cinema, although Frank Ripploh writing/directing/starring in his autobiographical film, *Taxi zum Klo*, was the most impressive personal expression from a cinematic perspective I witnessed. My favorite Los Angeles movies were *Killer of Sheep* and *The Exiles*. All I cared about was how movies could become like people. That was my dream: to link the idea of being a person with the idea of being a movie. I desired to become a person who made people movies, fusion of life and cinema, like happened in *Chungking Express, The Coca-Cola Kid, Hysterical Blindness, Millennium Mambo, Local Hero, Sweet Sixteen, Thirteen, Unknown Pleasures, Morvern Callar, Mala Noche*, the whole thing of Italian neorealism: *Bicycle Thieves, Il Posto, The Nights of Cabiria, Mammo Roma, Rocco and His*

Brothers, plus Yasujirō Ozu, from silent to color, all of Ozu— it's too late to say don't get me started, I already started, now I'll end. I promise there are many more movies which immerse the viewer in feelings of being a person alive in the actual present, movies about life, *Shadows in Paradise* for example, but I think I've illustrated that movies about the lives of people meant a tremendous deal to me. Watching movies about people, for example *Goin' Down the Road,* and *Naked,* plus *The Fireman's Ball,* the entire *Three Colors* trilogy, and some more I'm not mentioning, including *Slacker,* these movies were one of my favorite forms of hanging out with other people.

As mentioned earlier, an Ohio movie friend of mine moved to live in Orange County California with me, and within the ignorance and arrogance of youth we felt filled with massive dreams related to making movies, then our adulthood began and reality was different than our dreams (classic), and after moving to Los Angeles, moving to Portland, moving back to Los Angeles, then everything movie about my life was over, after for a long while movies had been what felt most important to me.

Sigh. In my past I traveled away from other roads at the end of which were other goals of mine, so when I left the idea of making movies I was adult enough to know that shit happens.

With certainty: the roads of cinema and the roads of books are within the same city. So I never strayed too far from books as I wrote scripts, as I didn't stray too far from movies while I wrote books—and I never cared much for roads, anyway.

In fact my life had only one road, which went like this: Tomorrow. Tomorrow, tomorrow, tomorrow. That was the road which would lead me to my end. On city sidewalks I thought about this and days behind me, days ahead of me, books I'd written, books I'd write.

Chapter Nine

Discussions concerning the core of this book, which is me, same-same but different as I was during other books I've written.

First of all, these words walk inside your head. At no point will these words materialize to strut before you. This writing doesn't constitute a reader's physical reality, these words compose a writer's verbal reality at the time of this writing.

Second of all, I'm not sure why I began the chapter that way, I think it was me becoming excited about mentioning something that seemed interesting to me at the time, but upon reflection that felt perhaps too blunt. Was I ever clued into the art of seduction? What was elegance to me, could I describe it, would I want to?

These words are an imitation of my life, except as I always said, *In life one doesn't get rewrites.* In terms of what I wrote of and what I didn't write of, there was what I wrote of and what I didn't write of. This all felt like a good idea at the time, and why would one want to write what doesn't feel like a good idea?

Always I enjoyed: writing about writing the book about my life I was living and writing about. My previous books? At their worst I'd already forgiven them. Did I adore them? Yes. Each one? Yes. My mistakes? Already over, and forgiving oneself for the things which might kill you is what helps one live. *Stormy Fortune* is another book about myself and my reality isn't nothing but love and noise, this book is about that and how I wait not for my days to pass but for my thoughts and feelings to sweep through me. It was both true that my emotions were inverse to my reality sometimes, and that my emotions could become my reality. Did I have anxiety? Only always. On occasion I was so keen to rationalize my anxiety. Almost as if sometimes I waited for my anxiety to prove itself, but there was a severe problem in terms of finding vs. creating anxiety, and on occasion my anxiety latched onto moments as if they were the assurances I craved, when in fact I could misread rooms, which could illustrate a cycle within my worries, of creating the problems I wanted to fight—and my emergency vessel perspective, built and saved for dire situations, was remembering that I had become familiar with problems, through finding and creating them.

Let me summarize the previous paragraph, which I'd like to leave there as is, in order to provide transparency toward how I reach summaries. Summary: I didn't write of my life to fix it, I wrote what I lived because I lived it, trying not to worry about what I had already worried about, for what I didn't worry of was what kept me sane enough to write, which made me feel happy enough to be alive. Writing gave me the nutrients I need to sustain my existence. If I could start a slogan it'd be *Write to Live*, but I couldn't start a slogan.

What I thought of while writing this book was writing this book, as what I thought of while living was being alive. If sometimes my words sound like not enough, let me mention, sometimes life was not enough, and sometimes not enough is better than too much, and sometimes I am too much, and sometimes life was too much.

My reality, how much of it was I learning of by taking long walks and reading, writing? Was I learning of literature, life, or myself? I was learning of myself and others within a world of words. Was there an advantage to that? Did not the world stay the same while I explored myself and words? It was that my life told me what I'd write about, and books told me how I'd write it. Outside these pages were computer screens and blue skies. Outside these pages was eternity and everything not mentioned. Inside these pages I threw my words into infinity. *Stormy Fortune*: thought narratives of a man who at times felt trapped in solitude but wrote about it. Myself, I liked reading about these things, people who wrote of being themselves were my favorite types of writers, like I've been saying, so everything about me was all right in my opinion. Everything happens how it happens.

Obvious: my human condition manifests itself through words, *Story Fortune* was meant to be a calming, self-nurturing meditation upon existence, written with thoughts outside a person, in word land, to exist within grace and feel as if already saved. This is a book about the types of things I tended to think about, a series of essays in relation to my existence as a Midwestern-Angeleno writer who every day was one day closer to death. One can tell how a person thinks about themselves based on how the person thinks about the world. So all the words in this book reflect me and my reality in some way or another, from either my id, ego, or superego (depending). And speaking of cosmic phantom strength, which I'd like to bring up, and paranoid rigid delusions... I never held anybody's reaction to their reality against them, including their reaction to the reality of me.

In my writing sometimes often I longed to explore dark chambers in my mind most of all. I wasn't certain of all the things inside these chambers which should be saved or discarded. I searched in dark chambers for things which I perhaps needed or could sell, journaling my search, and this was the type of stuff I treasured reading like I keep saying. Not about finding but searching. The flame of a search is snuffed by a find. I believed my search began at birth and will end at my death, my whole life a search for how I can make sense to this world. Will I ever explore the entirety of my mind's chambers? Impossible. Real talk: no one's soul is just words. No one's soul in finite. On top of that, when on some days I knew not the chambers I should explore, what I did was I made new chambers, in order to explore them. What turned on chamber lights and revealed to me the unseen? Additional real talk: the end of every paragraph I flip a light switch, yank a chain clap my hands or strike a match, do whatever needs done for giving light to darkness.

Human topic: never before the time in which this was written had the world been so wired into awareness, of other people and other cultures, amid Internet culture, which was how everyone was wired, everyone was plugged into the past and present and it all felt wild enough according to some but I hadn't thought it was any big deal really, since humans were still infants as far as I dreamed. But what happened was the creation of self-aware writing built upon the past. Wikipedia was a global exchange of knowledge. Google came to mean the same as Coca-Cola in a time when there were seven billion people alive, the most number of people ever—so of course there were more writers than ever, writers aware or capable of being aware of all the writers around them, and before them, but the dangerous question was if there were more readers than ever, and there were, because of the Internet, but I meant in terms of books. To know of life one must live, same as to know a book one must read.

As a writer of books I could adjust my perspective during each book I wrote—I could rephrase my reality—and my changed perspectives were reflections of my changing self, this I knew for sure. *Stormy Fortune* became itself based on what my life became, and my mother always told me that my thoughts compose my reality. If my thoughts composed my reality, let not my thoughts be of my worries. As thinking of what's bad makes one's life worse, how could it not be true that thinking of what's good makes one's life better? What's better than my life? Writing this book. My mother she said a lot of things and sometimes it was hard to listen to her but it was never hard for me to love her. She showed me a type of strength which I never witnessed in anyone else. My mother was a concept and my mother, and she was a writer too. This is another chapter dedicated to her and my sister. We all three knew well of the fight that our lives take.

While writing this book I thought about how I was writing this book. Then, big picture: I didn't even matter to the world, not even after my mother loved me! Just a fact. I didn't matter more than any other person, and there were seven and a half billion people. And so I would begin to ponder this, but I'd realize I was pondering what I always pondered and wasn't helpful like I've mentioned. I wasn't afraid of death but I was afraid of fucking up my life, and fear didn't help, never did, just like worry. Never did worry help, which has been mentioned, along with a mentioning of it having been mentioned. Because I'm just certain that it doesn't help.

By writing this book I desired to contribute to the land of words, which was bigger than me and everyone I knew. I would die and everyone I loved would die too, but these words stay in the land of words. It's readers who give words life. A reader: anyone/anytime. Readers trip out on what they trip out about. I couldn't find a lot of people to trip out on my writing but I knew there were a lot of people, a lot of time, and I knew the classic: *Art is long, life is short.* When I was alone in life I was only kind of alone, since not only was I with people while reading, but by writing I left parts of myself behind for others. *Stormy Fortune* is a rose petal I dropped along my path. Fact.

In the contemporary, both movies and the Internet hold cultural footprints of a greater size than the cultural footprint of books, but regardless, my books were only read by my family and friends (*Larry Angeles* the common favorite). And memoir writing was a dangerous form of literature, prone to accusations of narcissism and limited perspectives, hyperbolic egos, but that doesn't matter for now because what I thought about while writing this book was writing this book. While writing I monitored my pathos but, as I mentioned, every word in *Stormy Fortune* came from my ego, or id, or superego, while I searched for how I might fit within a book, building up to fitting within reality and, as I learned to say in Portland, *Trying my best here.* When I felt my life slipping, slipping, I grabbed ahold of words and whisper-screamed.

Chapter Ten

Exploring the enormity of learning everything and becoming a successful writer, which is related to ideas discussed in the previous chapter, except different, building from it.

He asked me, "Is it literature?"

He was asking about my writing. This was an art book store behind my apartment. Morgan and I had once brought our first set of poetry book proofs here, all three: *Frank Zappa & Barry Manilow, the name of this book is untitled but that's a bit of a lie,* and *Eudaimonia.* They had been imperfect proofs, dirty books, infant poetry, and we didn't hear back. When Morgan and I whipped our books into shape and ordered a new set of proofs, we brought them into the store again. We didn't hear back. When Morgan and I collected our three poetry books into *Basic Mutant Psychosis: Annals of Los Angeles 2014-2016,* all of this felt like moving forward for us at the time, though we moved toward a pit without planks, for we brought *Basic Mutant Psychosis* into the art book store and we didn't hear back. We visited again in order to leave our e-mails, and an e-mail was exchanged between me and the guy there, regarding it better to send over a PDF, and he wasn't sure where our proofs were. He said lots of people gave him proofs. Morgan and I decided we were trying. I sent the PDF. We never heard back nor had our proofs returned.

We dropped the first set of proofs off to a Russian art book store employee who once stayed a night in my apartment's living room, on a private cot, when she first moved to Los Angeles. We had met on the Internet and I cherished how she spoke of the world. So, three years after she moved to LA, eight months after Morgan and I had brought in our proofs while dreaming of beginning Neon Burrito Publishing, following *Cosmic Robotics* I had the idea to ask the Russian if she wanted to meet with me to talk about being published. She said she did and she asked for us to meet at the art book store. When I weighed the pros/cons of that situation I agreed, I met her there and we were talking about publishing a book of her writing—she'd brought in a journal of hers, which had random lists and strange scattered trinkets, clouds of thoughts about this and that, she asked me, "What do you think?" and I was amazed, her journal was like a person, I told her, "This is amazing"—though before I was talking to the Russian I was meeting the guy who turned out to be the guy who was supposed to receive the proofs Morgan and I had delivered eight months prior.

It was a curated store and he asked me, "Is it literature?" I didn't think the guy or the store seemed much into literature. I wasn't interested in getting into a conversation about what is and isn't literature, I said, "It's just writing." And his face was pleasant seeming, he was comfortable. I knew being self-published through CreateSpace wasn't going to earn me street cred. How did it get brought up? It did. I might have brought it up. And I said it was what I could afford, I said I wanted to make my books in some downtown place on my own in my own way. He asked me, "That's great. Where?" He thought I was saying I knew the place and was going to do that. I said, "I wish I knew. I can't find that place." UPCs were brought up—who for the love of hell brought up UPCs? In a state of panic I might have mentioned having UPCs and he was calm and I was there in life and things were going how they go. He said, "I don't even know if people need UPCs anymore." He fucking said that. I smiled and nodded—always the best response. He'd already been smiling, and then, after I'd talked with the Russian about her writing, which I wanted to publish (but later wouldn't, after she switched to graphic design), then I left for my apartment across Fairfax and a series of thoughts ran within me predicated upon the philosophy of YOLO, You Only Live Once, you know, I thought of that, or something like that, deeply, I felt a fire within my nature at that moment in my life and so I gathered together the Neon Burrito books I had in my apartment: *Larry Angeles, My Autobiography Is My Manifesto: Volume One, automanifest*, and *Cosmic Robotics*.

I was living without fear but that's not all it takes. I was being myself but that's not all it takes. I felt calm-enough but that's not all it takes.

I brought in, for proper consideration, the 8.5x11" *My Autobiography Is My Manifesto: Volume One.* Its large format and text had been the original concept and my idea. This book had personality inspired by my madness. This was my idea about what a fun book might be like, at the beginning of when

I was realizing I could make books. I was delighted that, "I can make any type of book now," and pretty much right in the beginning I became outrageous. When I brought *My Autobiography Is My Manifesto: Volume One* into the bookstore where I worked at the time, not the art book store but a different bookstore, a manager of my workplace said, "Did you order a proof?" I said, "There had been seven proofs." She said, "Oh." She nodded and smiled. She said maybe she was normcore but she didn't think it'd sell. She showed me an example of a better book. A professional book. A real book, compared to my silly thing, she was implying. Following that conversation was when I made the 5x8" version, *automanifest*. I had wanted to create a book which could be sold where I worked, so I had written of my past, since *Larry Angeles* mentioned me working at that store, which meant I couldn't imagine selling it there, and later *automanifest* did end up being sold where I worked. I worked in a bookstore where my book was being sold and that felt forward. *automanifest* in any size the concept was never an intimate hit with many people, except with a few choice people, which had been my writing career so far, and I'd call that all right.

So I was inside the art book store, which wasn't the bookstore where I worked, and the Russian and the store manager were looking at *My Autobiography Is My Manifesto: Volume One* with the kind-enough eyes for which I'd hoped. The Russian said, "Maybe the font is too big," but she didn't sound angry. They didn't seem upset while looking at the books. My biggest hope was they'd like my words. They didn't read much from my books. Turned pages. Polite faces. They handed me back my books. Nothing was said about anything and I left the art book store and the sun slapped me as I returned to my apartment, where I laid upon my bedroom futon. A thing I'd heard said was you can't count on nobody but yourself, and I tried to think of the ways in which I could count on myself, and I remembered that I could count on myself to keep writing, so writing became worth it and everything felt fine, when I started thinking about it like that, in order to feel better.

All that was last year, and this year, after Morgan had gotten our books into Skylight Books and Book Soup, which filled us with joy more than book sales, then in the middle of July I handed him, he had done illustrations for it, *Oscar Wilde's The Picture of Dorian Gray,* the book I'd written during a life period when I just fucking had to write a book (like now), I just had to, that was all it was, sheer necessity, plain spirit, and I handed him the book and we walked for a spell except we split off some bit after he told me he thought he should step away from Neon Burrito.

I returned to my room and wrote; my room disappeared and life became pages.

That was what I did and do. I had already started the book.

Stormy Fortune used to be titled *This guy does not die easily*, based on a line from *Q: The Winged Serpent*, which I had watched with my Ohio friend who lived down the street, down Melrose, next to Pink's Hot Dogs.

This book came from having learned again, again, again, that nothing was promised in life and one could wish for the best but expect nothing. Here was this thing which both books and people helped me realized: there was nothing unique about my pain or suffering, and there was nothing unique about mentioning it either. Feeling stuck was just a fundamental responsibility attached to the human condition, shared by many. My existential battle was within me and I wanted to think of other things in my life but not much in my reality reminded me of the myself I wanted to become. When did I feel like the world—when every worry was understandable, everything was just what we were going through then.

A(another) circumstance of mine in terms of how I was developing as a professional writer was I hadn't previously imagined myself developing a network of writer friends, the same I hadn't imagined myself becoming a writer through business. I never thought that writing came from anywhere but writing. I imagined myself becoming a writer because I thought of knowing and caring for the game of words, which game accepts any person has no rules and isn't actually a game, but something like art, impartial and magnificent, both distant and private, words, and what I imagined in my head was that was most important anyway, my belief in words, my belief in writing the words I wrote at the time I did how I did, my wordy belief nesting inside each word I wrote, which sort of conviction exists among writers who are readers, and felt important to me. And I'd thought about this far more than I'd thought about how to make friends.

No one was telling me to write, but I kept writing. "If you build it, they will come." The voice in *Field of Dreams*, a 1989 movie which manifested the American dream, which movies could do when they wanted to.

For *Oscar Wilde's The Picture of Dorian Gray* I had begun to think that I could better clarify my situation regarding my life and infinite possibility. I felt like I could make my feelings regarding infinite possibility clearer. One aspect of infinite possibility is infinite sadness. I read other fine books regarding emotional doom and gloom. I read them most of all. And I thought that when it was clear through my words how my life felt, it would be clear that I could write. Since I'd clarified myself. And this would be a symbol of my personal strength. But that was coming from an illusion my thoughts created regarding just how much people like reading of other people's personhood. The world always asks: *How much of you is worth being shared?* Life on its own illustrates the ingredients of doom and gloom, and it was reading from other books while continuing to be my (same)self which enabled me to write of my (same)self in a different way, based on having already written *Oscar Wilde's The Picture of Dorian Gray,* based on others books I read and more life experience around people: *Stormy Fortune.*

Summary: *Stormy Fortune* is prose composed in a human form, an expression of ripe character, as *Oscar Wilde's The Picture of Dorian Gray* was, but those were other days with other thoughts, moments and books between me then and me now.

For example, from a practical perspective, after Neon Burrito published *Oscar Wilde's The Picture of Dorian Gray* I offered to mail, and did mail, that book to several other writers. Now, I had been so excited about the enterprise of publishing that book, on June 13th, that I ordered 13 physical copies but, of course (ughck), I spotted about 13 typos in the first printing, which had already happened, and I was prepared to give 13 people a copy, including other writers.

No fear (but that's not all it takes). Every typo I noticed upon inspection bummed me out and rushed me to my computer for correction (natural), but I've never met a typo which destroyed my book or life. Typos were uh-ohs and I'd heard of bigger problems. There were 13 reasons everything was gonna go bad and only 1 (mystery) reason it might go well.

Most writers I became friends with on Facebook pulled away from me over a short period of time and without much interaction, since interactions I did have were often followed by me not feeling comfortable, for whatever reason, usually. I was both repulsed by tribal culture and aware of its advantages —I both fought against it and strove for it. Yet I so often drifted from the possible connections I could forge with other people. Gave up. Couldn't figure it out. Felt like a way different type of person. Wanting to be like no one I ended up being with no one, although this myth I kept hearing was change is inevitable and it'll all work out in the end.

The one writer I heard back from was Scott McClanahan—

Shawn—Just wanted to let you know I read *Oscar Wilde's The Picture of Dorian Gray* and I loved it. Like really loved it. Seems like the only books that interest me now are books about writing the book the reader is reading. Love the part about you and Morgan deciding to write a book so you can have a reading at Skylight. The fragments are great too. You reference Sebald in the novelette and I was thinking before I came to that part. This feels like a newer version of Sebald. And yes memory is nothing unless it's death. Anyway, I really loved it and it felt refreshing and I hope you keep doing stuff like this because it is really needed.

The 13 ways a thing could go bad often came my way, and I thought they always could, but 1 other person could be a good thing that came my way too.

Chapter Eleven

Reflections culminate regarding personal emotions initiated at least two chapters ago; this illustrates my nature.

[Note to self] Consider this: Now means not the same thing as Forever—and what the fuck about Forever applies to me?

[Note to self] Tidy this philosophy: all I had was all I needed.

[Reminder to self] Ambrose Bierce's definition of a Cynic within *The Devil's Dictionary*:

> A blackguard whose faulty vision sees things as they are, not as they ought to be. Hence the custom among the Scythians of plucking out a cynic's eyes to improve his vision.

[Personal realization:] Oh, okay—reality can be fucking hilarious, like dark humor. And life means more than laughs, but at the very least life means some laughs.

[I'm] Building things up like this for a mysterious reason which feels necessary to me now (oh I remember why, as a method for introducing the concept of writing flowering in my mind during my years alive), headed toward mentioning: no rules on a page, like I've mentioned. No rules but customs and elaborations upon customs, and the dance between people and words. What I cared about was each writer's dance—shake it up! Let loose! Feel free! Simply: when one dances there is the question of how one dances, anyone can dance how they want to dance, that has been the essence of writing since Forever. This dance of mine is titled *Stormy Fortune* and here I was dancing in the rain, dancing in the rain, dancing in the goddamn rain—I've been dancing in the rain for some time, and I'll keep dancing as Robyn mentioned I should, in that song of hers, "Dancing On My Own".

Summary: my life was a tap dance atop reality, same as my life was a tap dance atop theses pages. I appreciated that I felt mostly alone while I lived and yet here in this book I was in full exhibition for a reader's potential viewing pleasuring. You're watching me dance and that's golden because I'll be dancing regardless. For the sake of the performance. For the sake of words. For the sake of everything, for my own sake, like I've been saying.

I adored that in art one was permitted to do anything, so everyone just wondered if that was a good idea. That was the best way to create art, I thought: From Anything/Into Anything. This was my favorite type of character personality: someone capable of doing anything. I didn't most relate to people who were always-good or always-bad, I most related to the always-wild.

As a person I lived in total wonder, as writers always have and will—what the fuck else would writers do with all their wonder? Rather write than worry. Writers are people who know that people can create anything they want to create, anything can be imagined. Writing is just a matter words. The best form of written art was called literature, and I adored it, based on principle. And this was true too: everyone created their own art, no matter what one called it. As much as I desired the best of anything I was egalitarian.

As earlier mentioned, at the time of this writing everyone was wired into the Internet, enabling awareness about what was being written and had already been written—and I knew that life's crucial topics, worthy of consideration, most everything had already been written of, some of it best mentioned by the Greeks in Western culture, so it went, so it keeps going. As a writer I hoped to explore what my writing could become, in terms of no one having been like me, like this, this way, my way, I became myself, I was the only I like this, and I was not better than the rest but I had idiosyncratic curiosities which I transmitted into my life and life perspective, shit which gripped me and spun my days, shit which tripped me out and allowed me to imagine myself being pulled within interior realms of reader/writerly human understanding, still believing/ always believing that one learns of life from life—and this was the type of shit I liked reading about, for real.

I first understood words as a way of experiencing life—*Stormy Fortune*. So that covers that and what was covered was how I see the things I mentioned.

That song, Drama Duo, "Forever's Gone":

Because you see
You see what you want to see
You believe what you want to believe

You see what you want to see
You believe what you want to believe
There's no other way

Because I'm not afraid
to be alone
to be alone

Some people find life most comfortable within what has already been discovered and explained to them. Why was anything new needed when the past was perfect? All anyone ever missed was their childhood, anyway. In a June 5, 2017 article, producer Matt Tolmach was quoted by Hollywood Reporter as saying:

That is the conundrum of where we're living right now: People want what feels familiar, but they don't want it to be familiar.

After I shared the first chapter of *Stormy Fortune* with the person who made the cover to *Oscar Wilde's The Picture of Dorian Gray*, he told me:

This is probably my favorite passage that I've read from any of your work. Your writing, when it's explicitly autobiographical, has a tendency toward being distracting, self-conscious, ironically opaque. But somehow you writing about any random thing outside yourself has a way of turning on all the lights and throwing open the curtains. The more you write about whatever random things, places, or concepts interest you at that moment in time, the more I feel like your writing is letting me know you.

[Quotes me.]

I mean, come on. That's so, so good. That's like your id just drafted its mission statement.

Then I felt prompted to confess to him my desire to move away from my purity, considering my earlier writing pure, and my new writing impure, as happens when a person transitions from being born to becoming an adult, which was the traditional experience of human life and the life of writers. Within the world of words my puberty was public. Human nature. How many of the books I'd written were exactly like the other? Zero. They all chat about the same shit, but each one was its own literary journal from my life, growing from some idea I had about myself and writing at the time when I wrote it.

I changed as a person goddamn right in front of people—and who cared? I cared.

At the time when this chapter was being written, it had been four months since *Oscar Wilde's The Picture of Dorian Gray* had been published. I used to be able to count on my friends and family as readers, but I was beginning to lose my number of friend and family readers, which I understood. I sometimes wondered of the number of people I lost purely from *My Autobiography Is My Manifesto: Volume One*, which I adored for its innocence, I've mentioned it, and: biased. I could see how that book would seem as if perhaps a lapse in certain faculties related toward creating mature, professional forms of art. But, the criticisms I had heard and imagined (paranoid), most of them missed the feeling intended from the creation of an adult-children's book, which I wanted to behave exactly as if an adult-child. Eff rules. No fear. No profession. Nothing but innocence and character. That book was me coming my closest toward creating some type of Venice Beach Self-Transformation book, powered by some interior engine, fashioned by my own design.

Was I a person who wanted to be associated with some type of Venice Beach Self-Transformation book? Yes. Why not? I didn't see the problem. That is the category where I would place what became *automanifest*, a coming-of-age novelette written with poetic-type prose, a fine-tuned 5x8" version of *My Autobiography Is My Manifesto: Volume One*, though I published *automanifest* without capital letters, still behaving mostly like a child, knowing every adult rule I obeyed would only quiet my inner child (Fuck That, I felt at the time). I didn't believe that rule following would be a proper presentation of my radical youth persona. Plus here's this book too, fanatical self-forged ideologies from the first person. There are other books. There was all of me, the pure and the impure.

Adult Gummies by K. Karivalis would be published by Neon Burrito mid-November. I read its final draft; it was written by a person who lived in the same world as me, same time—different eyes. I treasured my reading experience. She had precision, which always I appreciated. I imagined her in a section of literature named Mellow Existentialism. Hers would be the first book published by someone unknown to me in the physical world. She was a memer—what happened was the creator of the *Larry Angeles* cover, Christina Gubala, messaged me that Karivalis was her favorite memer and was writing a book, mentioning that I should publish her. I was delighted to become able to publish Karivalis, feeling grateful for meeting her and having read *Adult Gummies.*

Here's a difference between things: if I were living in Ohio and I told you, "Hey, I'm living the dream," you'd say "Prove it," is my guess. But I lived in Los Angeles, and one might begin by believing I was living the dream, if I told them I was. I was trying to tell myself. Like I've said: in this city life isn't guaranteed to become your dream, but one's dream becomes one's life for many. As far as I knew, the dream in fact lived in Hollywood Hills. Are not our dreams above us? The glow of this dream was cast upon Hollywood, and some people lived within the glow. But there were all these other parts of this city which was massive and contained many neighborhoods. A lot of the dream lived in Malibu, near the ocean. I lived in Mid-City West, a section which was nothing exceptional as I mentioned in the beginning. Beverly Grove, who cared, I cared. I have mentioned Ambrose Bierce said this in another way: each moment each person is only the person they are in that moment.

Always forward, that was what the dark kids said to conquer their fears during the time this was being written. The days behind me were done, the days ahead of me remained. Had I lived half my life yet? As Cicero said in another way: life was terrible the whole way through, but when it was over it was over. What would my worries be when I was dead? Zero worries then. So as rough as my days could feel to me, they were all okay enough to be my days, and sometimes I would rather not worry, though sometimes I felt honest about many worries, each of everything a piece of my life's totality.

Patience was a virtue I kept my eyes on as I aged, sometimes looking away by accident. The more I learned the more I knew how much I didn't know. I could become impatient with myself. I could become overwhelmed by how much there was to learn. Always the same me. Managing the line between a physical and spiritual world. Sometimes feeling as if everyone living their lives was getting in my way. As if everyone was an obstacle. Blaming other people for being obstacles. But I was learning as I aged that I gave each person a reality, and they gave me one back. Oh, I gave other people my reality. But by learning more of another person I learned more of their reality, and by learning of other realities I learned more of my own, I knew, I felt, every day I had to remember that, when I started having pissy thoughts. Everyone had their own fight.

Mostly I read books about what being a person was like. I moved to Los Angeles thinking of the world as massive, anything possible, learning through experience that the world and the city could turn against me, and time after time I felt as if nothing was possible. The world was larger and stranger than my large and strange dreams, I realized within Los Angeles. A thing I held inside myself was a constant feeling of actually being utterly insignificant to existence: carried this within me, always, some small part ready to give this whole gig up. Sometimes that part of me was large and sometimes that part of me was small. While writing this book that part of me was small. A certain poem within *Eudaimonia* was probably the most depressing thing I'd published. It didn't seem possible to me that my life could become just anything. Only a little bit of all of life would be possible for me, I figured out. I could only become who I was. And I wasn't who I wanted to be. This world wasn't what I wanted it to be. So my life was not about wanting, it was about becoming.

[Note to self]: Light as a feather stiff as a board, but in terms of philosophy.

[A difference between me and a scientist]: For each human, the universal was personal.

Chapter Twelve

A chapter related to old and new friends.

Lately I'd been calling my longtime friends who knew how to sing the blues with me. We learned to sing along back in high school days.

But when I called them and sang them my song of now, they each said, "Wow," and they each fell silent.

I told my old friend/still friend Richard that I'd feel content if I didn't become homeless. How would I rescue myself? Who was there for me? What was there for me in life? If I became doomed, I'd be doomed. Richard, a public prosecutor, the most pro-criminal prosecutor he knew, he aimed for the lightest sentences possible, the other prosecutors he knew were pro-law, after I sang my blues to him he said he was sorry but he didn't expect me to say that and he didn't know what to say. We couldn't any longer sing the blues together. Not that he didn't have his own blues, but we didn't have the same blues. He told me that sometimes at random he'd find himself wondering if he should just die. And he found chatting with me difficult!

Richard told me he sometimes wondered if being better meant being dead, and he said I depressed him. I hadn't spoken of a sunny side to life, that's true.

The other person I called to sing the blues with was John, who had become a father, and what was most important to John was his daughter, which I thought was totally awesome. John and I basically had nothing in common, he was a computer programmer in Seattle, he lived with his daughter's mother and the mother's two other sons, but John would always listen to me, even when he knew not what to say, and he never made me feel worse, for even when I would tell him what could bring him down, and exhaust him, he would feel not down and exhausted by me but by our conversation. He had been a longtime, good friend, and I wrote about our year's previous trip to Las Vegas in *Cosmic Robotics*. And still my blues left him speechless. He brought up some problems he'd been experiencing as a new home owner, and considerations he was having regarding home schooling his daughter or not.

So I had two phone friends who I couldn't always call and sometimes I would feel as if I had no one to call, no one to see. I could feel perfectly alone in the world. Within Los Angeles there were a few people I knew and could see, under certain circumstances. Morgan had moved to live with his significant other in a place where Peter Lorre once lived (Morgan heard), and he was happy in his relationship and I was happy he was happy, although I didn't see him much. In the recent, since July, I saw him once at Steve's new luxury apartment on Hollywood Boulevard. We spent our time in the living room and the third-floor patio. The patio faced the innards of the apartment complex and I felt as if within a Polish movie or something like that, which I mentioned and Morgan agreed. In the past, some of *Gooses* had been shot outside a room once rented by Steve in Hollywood Hills. I always appreciated how and where Steve chose to live. I knew Morgan from California but I knew Steve from Ohio. Steve had converted his mom's backyard shack into a party palace that was well-known in our high school days. For that matter, I, with other friends, experienced multiple lovely nights sleeping in the back of Steve's SUV at a wooded campsite in Ohio. His SUV had a television for *NFL Blitz*. We would open the back windows and let the night spill in. The night would overtake us and we would feel light, as we had wanted to feel during the day. That summer we listened to The Unicorns, "Who Will Cut Our Hair When We We're Gone?". We told each other stories from our days, our wishes for our lives, and we were all young enough to feel that everyone was being perfectly reasonable. Also, I had lived with Steve on W. 10th St. in Long Beach, California, and those days I mentioned in *automanifest* as golden days. Steve was handsome like a movie star and he was one of the nicest people I knew. That night in Los Angeles, in his luxury apartment on Hollywood Boulevard, Steve was an exceptional host. He, Morgan, and I ate pizza while listening to music and chatting, catching up, sharing some emotions, and then we watched Erik Skjoldbjærg's *Insomnia*.

There was what was inside of me, and there was what was beside me, and Dave was beside me, trapped inside himself. He was driving down Western, it was afternoon and California sunlight licked the streets. We were returning from a chiropractor, where we picked up *Afterglow (a dog memoir)*, which Dave had left behind by accident, and in the car while driving he said to me, "Is it bad to be wanted?" Women he'd been seeing hadn't been wanting him. He told me he wanted someone to care for him. I was a romantic and dreamed of relationships where people took care of each other, but I knew what Dave was saying, felt him on that. Certainly I hadn't wanted Dave to feel alone. I could relate. Dave wanted anyone who would take care of him and I wanted someone whom I hadn't met and couldn't describe.

An hour later we'd be in Dave's neighborhood and drive past this neighbor friend of his. This neighbor I'd heard of more than I'd come to know, an older guy who I'd heard liked me and my friends whom Dave hung around with, which this neighbor mentioned to Dave, who mentioned it to me. That day when we passed the neighbor and he saw us he said to me, "Hey Larry," as we drove by waving. I hadn't responded to what he'd said though I'd been waving, but I guessed what Dave told me, which was the neighbor had been mentioning my novella *Larry Angeles.* "He's read it," I asked Dave who said, "Yes." Then Dave said, "That book saved my life," which was a thing he told me before and which I treasured to hear, although Dave was a nice guy who said nice things which could be nicer than true. But his story was that he'd gone to Palm Springs with his friend, and he and his friend weren't getting along, so Dave on his phone read the PDF of *Larry Angeles,* which he would say was exactly what he needed then. Whether the book in fact saved his life is an irrelevant detail compared to how nice a thing that was for him to tell me.

Dave was the most recent good friend I'd acquired in life. He was a decade and a half older than me and was as confused about the world as I was. Our friendship was a rocky road but I treasured him. He was my referral for what became my new job.

From my old job, at the book store, more than three people had left just before I would. One was a receiving room manager who had been nice-enough to me, he was mentioned within *Larry Angeles*, he was an Ohioan so I missed him after he left, based on principle. Before him another person left, for Austin, Texas, I ate with her at Canter's on her final day. We ate with another co-worker friend who became promoted as Assistant Manager at Grauman's Egyptian Theatre. Another person who left was an older married man with a teenaged daughter. He handed me his resignation letter, to hand to a manager, saying he'd never been treated so terrible while paid so little. This was the business buzzword then: Metrics. His metrics had been questioned. Metrics were, no doubt, invented by Satan. And I heard from other co-workers that they wanted to leave: actors waiting for their parts, students waiting to finish school, and just in general some people wanted to leave from having decided not to become lifers where we worked. Some people left because of the cost of living in a city—one person returned to her home in the Valley, the land of suburbs outside Los Angeles, but one special day she returned to visit the store, and give me my first tarot card reading. Her friend gifted me my first crystal. They had taken the train to visit. Most people I worked with didn't know what having a lot of money was like. We were people who liked few things since we could afford few things. I would be leaving the store for a new job. I was ready. I knew it would be easier for the book store to replace me than it would be for me to replace the store, in terms of giving a fuck. At that job I and all the others had been cogs in a corporate wheel, that was the reality of that job. The corporate world doesn't quite treasure human stuff, especially my kind of human stuff, though each person I worked with and encountered I treasured as a person, based on principle. I was a people person who just happened to be terrible at being around people. Leaving from the bookstore would feel for me like leaving my childhood behind, which one must, and my new job would still relate to books, from a more adult perspective, and what I'm building up to saying is that from the store I would most miss Maggie and George.

Then I was inside a Silver Lake house I'd never been inside before, it was Emma's birthday and there she was, it was Jacqui's house and there she was, there was her husband Murray, and there was Alex with Tal. We went out to eat some appetizers but returned to eat chicken pot pies which Jacqui had baked with monograms correlating to each of our names. For example, mine had an "S". Before dinner we chatted about

Phillip K. Dick and discussed whether *Do Androids Dream of Electric Sheep?* was better than *Blade Runner*, which Murray said it sure wasn't, since Philip K. Dick was a lousy writer, Murray said, and Emma mentioned some defensive statements regarding the process of creating sci-fi versus standard fiction, the cognitive wheels being dissimilar, she mentioned, noting that she appreciated Dick's form of writing for what it was. I mentioned I was on Emma's side because I was and it was her birthday and things happen when people talk about books and movies, agreements and disagreements are forged, relationships are altered, we were the type of people who thought this type of stuff was always a blast, and what I brought up though was how Dick lived in Santa Ana when he died, he was an Orange County writer, that was a sort of detail which I liked to mention, and was my way of diverting the conversation from further discussion regarding the ideological methods implemented toward an evaluation of Dick. Over dinner we chatted about VR and augmented reality, T.J. Miller, Jennifer Aniston, and Tal asked his phone, "Where can I hide a dead body tonight?" Which question Alex said might get him in trouble with the government she thought, but it was friction of a variety which gave us all smiles. Emma had brought her own birthday cake, which had blue icing with "Mark Wahlberg" written on top in pink. I ate a slice and I ate about seven scoops of three different types of ice cream.

The place with the highest concentration of people I tended to get along with was the gas station on the corner of Beverly and Fairfax. I would visit the gas station in the morning, in the afternoon, in the evening, purchasing various caffeinated drinks, chocolate milk, and candy bars. These people saw me every day for brief little bits during which time we smiled and nodded and sometimes asked about each other's day.

On occasion I visited my Ohio friend who lived down Melrose next to Pink's Hot Dogs. The one I'd been to school and lived with twice before. The one I knew since days in Ohio when we dreamed of what our lives could become. He lived with Megan and they were both like me, they both looked out into the world and wondered how it was possible that they were seeing what they were seeing. *This was reality!?* Sometimes I sat with them at their place, chatting and listening to music, appreciating being around each other. They lived in the same world I did, and we saw many things the same way. What did all three of us want? The mellow. No, yes, it was that easy to say what we wanted, the mellow, which does not dismiss the fight, but was a reaction against it, the mellow. What we wanted was not easy to get, that was what the world had taught each of us. The most recent time I visited them Michael was there. I knew Michael from California but we were both from Ohio, and when I saw him what I told him was, "You were in my high school yearbook, I'm positive." I met him six years prior to this night, after I returned to Los Angeles from Portland. We figured we'd seen each other maybe forty, fifty times, and I felt as if I'd known him for as long as I'd known my old friend, whose name was Karl Kendrick Kellawan III by the way. Karl was how I met Michael. Karl was how I met Megan. Karl was how I met Dave. Karl was how I met Damon. Damon hasn't been mentioned yet. Karl was how I met other people who haven't been mentioned. He would sometimes speak to me as no one else spoke to me, as if he not only agreed with me, but knew me. Even when he disagreed with me he sounded as if he knew me. And that would feel nice. We'd gotten into plenty of fights through the years, there'd been copious sulking from each of us throughout our history, but our friendship became the kind that kept going, and lasting friendships are not easy friendships to find, as far as I could tell. Neither of us had mastered the adult world. Neither of us had found a permanent shape within the adult world. Both of us at times felt as if our lives were slipping away from us. Both of us were only getting older. And we already knew the world wouldn't be easy. We had both learned that the world wouldn't be easy. We knew that. We were learning that we had to become easier on ourselves and those around us. Which we found easier to say than do. We found everything in life easier to say than do, as we kept saying. Everything was easy but life. But it was life we wanted.

Chapter Thirteen

Staring into the horizon, as one must.

Some people meditate or see a psychiatrist but I headed nowhere across sidewalks while exploring mysterious inner realms.

This tiny life problem I had, nearing me toward death, badly affecting me in other ways, was I started smoking again because that inspired me to do more walking. It was this game I played with myself where I quit smoking to begin smoking to quit smoking to begin smoking again, in order to show myself that I could smoke and not smoke. At the beginning of the year I had quit for a long haul, which had felt horrible to me, horrible, but later every time I quit I quit like that. I decided to smoke again when I wanted to, based on if my life situation warranted the interior reflections generated by smoking combined with the power of sidewalks. The sun in Los Angeles was nice but the sun was too much, the sun was emotionally manipulative, unlike the cool and quiet moon. I most enjoyed cruising across Beverly Grove sidewalks in the night, I've said this before. When my mornings arrived my days would start rough (always), but by night my days had already happened, the day was behind me, the adult world's eyes were closed, and every night I returned to reading or writing again, that and/or smoking/not smoking on sidewalks while caught in the swirl of my thoughts.

My new job began and there was a perspective adjustment I had to make regarding myself in this world, who I was, who I needed to be, who I could be, who other people wanted me to be, what the adult world wanted of me, what human emotions wanted of me, all these things I needed to examine and calibrate according to the world I learned of as I lived within it. I hadn't quite mastered the skill of getting along with people or making my life any easier. Did I desire to horribly alienate myself and die of fear alone? That hadn't been a particular desire of mine, so I was working on some personal issues I had in regard to what the world needed and wanted from me, and who I could be.

I had been reading, from Melville House's The Neversink Library, Mary MacLane's *I Await the Devil's Coming*:

> We think we progress wonderfully in the arts and sciences as one century follows another. What does it amount to? It does not teach us the all-why. It does not let us cease to wonder what it is that we are doing, where it is that we are going.

The subsequent paragraph begins:

> The arts and sciences go on and on—still we wonder. We have not yet ceased to weep.

Mary MacLane had been 19 years old, back in 1901 when she wrote her published journal. Her journal allowed her to escape from her life, she mentioned, and me, over one hundred years later, I could relate to her. Totally. Her descriptions of her thoughts—*peripatetic philosophy* (my philosophy was palate cleansing). I envied the depth of emotions she conveyed (the fervor of her youth). I imagined I might have written this entire book differently if I began it after finishing *I Await the Devil's Coming*, or if I had been Mary MacLane.

Do people read older books to collect facts? I read older books to revisit spirits which become alive through words, their time becoming my time, their eyes becoming my eyes, and there I was, all those days after they'd written of their lives, their spirits taking life in thoughts they gave me. My life could feel to me as if taking place not in the present but in the land of words, which spanned time and space, and I could live there with comfort as a reader and writer.

The thing is, every book I read appeared to help grow my perspective in some way. Sometimes in big ways. I couldn't help it: reading memoirs electrified my human sense of self. I was magnetized by personal writing which grew out from the writer. After Mary MacLane, did I travel back to Marie Bashkirtseff? No, I traveled forward, to *The Diary of Anaïs Nin: Volume One 1931-1934*.

> Literature is an exaggeration, a dramatization, and those who are nourished on it (as I was) are in great danger of trying to approximate an impossible rhythm. Trying to live up to Dostoevskian scenes every day.

I'm not saying I knew for certain that women were better at writing about being human, I'm just saying that had been my suspicion for a while. Men tend to concentrate on being better than human—and how often they fail. All the many ways Anaïs Nin described Henry Miller utterly fascinated me. What a full spectrum of emotions a human relationship entails. I liked when she wrote sassy things about him:

> Henry has nothing to be bitter about. Why does he
> continue to fight the world? He loves war for its own sake.
> He lives in an animal world, in which life is full but
> without directive power or a fully-awakened self-
> consciousness.

Then she later wrote of him:

> Henry breaks all the molds, all the forms, all the shells, all
> the edifices of art, and what is born is warm and imperfect.
> It is human.

I wasn't reading Henry Miller I was reading Anaïs Nin, and before then about him she said kinder things, meaner things, all things. I imagined I would've written *Stormy Fortune* differently if I began it after finishing *The Diary of Anaïs Nin: Volume One*, or if I had been Anaïs Nin. Though I hadn't finished reading that book even by the time I finished writing this one. I read long sections from it because I felt a thirst. I was so sure that reading it would improve my writing perspective that I started reading from it before I finished *I Await the Devil's Coming*, and I haven't yet mentioned Eileen Myles and *Chelsea Girls*. I haven't finished the latter book either, but I started it after I met the author. What was Eileen Myles like? So calm, I felt. So leveled. So reasonable. Not even all wild and crazy like I had guessed writers might be. It turns out that you can do wild and crazy things without being a wild and crazy person. Sensible people all the time write of irrational people and being irrational. Perhaps because I was a more irrational person was why I didn't seek much sense within my life or even within my books. A coherent perspective and clean prose were concessions I made for the readers. As I've mentioned in another book: really my dream would be to write all wild and crazy. Pure emotion; hope springs eternal. Except not only did I age as a reader and a writer, but as a person I realized that refusing to leave from the wild and crazy into any sense of coherence was too easy. Life: wasn't easy. I wanted life. Life was capable of coherence. There was reason in science. There was a reason everyone was human. Everyone wanted to be allowed to be wild and crazy, which was why the more difficult path was to be reasonable. Me, I searched for a clean perspective within my life, an understanding of my days, while being wild and crazy, and sometimes feeling how others often feel, which Eileen Myles mentioned in *Chelsea Girls:*

> Everything I did was something to fix me. With all my
> heart I was trying to be dead.

Life can feel as if pushing one toward a nothingness which equals death. And now I'll mention initial readings from Elizabeth Ellen's *Person/A*, and I'll emphasize the point being that every book I read made me wish my life had been different I had been different other things had taken place and I had written the book I was reading and lived the life of that writer instead of my life and what I'd written and I could almost begin to wish I had written something else, when I was feeling pissy about myself, which I could, when I compared myself to others. But on some days I'd read my writing and find parts of myself within my words which had been the point since the beginning. It might not all have been adding up to a professional career but it was certainly a lot of words adding up to me, and I couldn't say for sure why I was myself but I could say for sure that I was stuck being myself.

What of the world was I wondering besides my place within it —not one thing, but everything, as much as I could while I lived, sure okay yeah. And I was some tired cat aging in my apartment. Most people were unaware of me and I was unaware of what it meant it to be a person, but I was wildly wondrous and therefore fell under the spell of wanting to be aware of what being myself felt like and meant. Life was tricky and during those days everyone knew it, talked about it mucho. I had some things to say myself.

So I felt pushed forward and days kept pushing me forward and sometimes I felt pushed back and I couldn't figure out how to write my life as well as I could figure out how to write this book. Like I said in another book, I wrote because writing never judged me. Only I could judge myself while I wrote, and I could become hard on myself, but I could forgive myself too. I once told a person, "I didn't wait for someone to tell me I'm a writer." The person smiled and later told me a story related to people needing to be honest and aware of when they weren't writers.

Simply, while I was alive in this world, there I was living, it was all outrageous, it was all I had. On my strongest days I thought life was marvelous. On my weakest days I thought the world was filth and I was too. Fuck the world fuck me fuck everything I could get like that. Because it could all feel so meaningless. All the everyday tiny pitfalls could feel as if not worth it, resulting in personal suffering which wasn't helpful. Dealing with being myself was my daily challenge, the challenge I knew best. One day everyone I loved would be dead, like I said, and I hoped to die first, I'm mentioning.

Outside the glory and beauty of science exists the glory and beauty of the unreasonable, which I say exists within our human condition, and it was mostly there where I lived as both a person and a writer. Everything that should be done would be done, I hoped, and I most wanted to do what shouldn't be done. That was me. I was granted the dignity of doing this from the sacredness of writing.

Saying it like this: *Stormy Fortune* was a new home I built within the land of words. Here it stays forever. I believed that what I'd done was create a neighborhood of houses in the land of words, each home reflecting my life perspective at the time the house was built. I was the architect. I did the interior design. I was the landscape artist. I genuinely think, in terms of mathematics and human possibility, like I've been saying, readers exist for me. I knew for sure that I existed, you know. I'm just a fucking human. Every day, one day at a time, on my way toward death.

My existence was on the same planet as all these other people, my days existed within the same solar revolutions as everyone who lived while I did, and in my dreams my days were nowhere near the end days for all human beings. What were humans going to be in the future? Humans. This I promise: in the future I'd be the same person I am now. If it were the past, I'd be the same person I am now. What would I be doing in these time periods? Wow. Totally different things I bet. Maybe the things would have nothing in common. Or maybe no matter when or where I was I'd be writing. Any version of me would feel as if living alone, would be my guess. That dark garden in my soul, which I brought up a couple of times earlier. I knew it was there. I didn't live within it, it lived within me. The dark gardens were in font of those houses I mentioned, the ones with dark chambers I explored, like I was saying.

You (the reader) give me anxiety sometimes, as I try to explain myself, but I remember and you can remember that my anxiety is my anxiety and your anxiety is your anxiety. Always I felt safest when I imagined writing to myself, though I didn't write to leave me behind for myself. But I would if I had to and I already did.

What begins at the end of this book, going forward, headed where… And I wondered another thing that was unrelated. By the end of writing this it was October 29 and what next? This I didn't wonder, I knew: October 30. Then it would be Halloween and Halloween was my favorite holiday. Non-religious, non-national. Halloween was a holiday sin. A pagan holiday. That was the day this book would be published. Another thing I wondered was the day I would begin my next book, and what my next book would be, now that I finished this one. When my days were over my books would be too. My days were not over yet. Besides my days and besides my writing, I didn't know what would happen. My soul wished for more than days and writing. I would keep reading and it takes more than that. I would keep living, finger crossed, and it takes more than that. While it said too much, *Stormy Fortune* said not enough. I'd never say enough to be done writing, my whole life was a search, and I couldn't seem to find my shape within the adult world, which made my potential fulfillment of The American Dream seem unreachable, but—I've already said all this, this all sounds like me—I never wanted to be inside anyone else's dreams, I had my own dreams. No one asked me to be a writer, no one read me, no one called me a writer, and it takes more than that.

Feeling light, dreaming
Know why I should
Don't know why I shouldn't

It was nighttime when this book was done. Another book. Another book! Outrageous. The only business sense I had was in my dreams. I wiggled a foot and a fan was on while I finished typing from my futon. Blue drapes oscillated from the wind. I heard *swooshes* from Fairfax traffic. I felt the same at the end of this book as I felt at the beginning of this book. Except now I had written it. And this all felt like a good idea at the time, as it does every time I do this. Why do I live, why do I write again (again I say), the answer is in the question. This chapter is dedicated to my mother and sister. I tended to repeat what had meaning to me. I wanted to mention everything that I wanted to mention. And have I already mentioned the part about my new dream being to find a path toward living alone in some place where I can work to pay my bills and live to write. Because I just thought of that. What did I want from the world anymore but the bare necessities, one hundred books to read, a computer to write upon, and the quietness of lonely nights, away from the bossy sun and long days.

Beverly Grove

July-October 2017

xx

www.ingramcontent.com/pod-product-compliance
Lightning Source LLC
Chambersburg PA
CBHW030809180526
45163CB00003B/1210

* 9 7 8 0 9 9 8 5 2 0 5 3 7 *